Ranger Rick's NatureScope

AMAZING MAMMALS
PART II

National Wildlife Federation

Chelsea House Publishers
Philadelphia

This Chelsea House edition of NatureScope® with permission of Learning Triangle Press, an imprint of McGraw-Hill.

First published in hardback edition ©1999 Chelsea House Publishers.

Library of Congress Cataloging-in-Publication Data

Amazing mammals / National Wildlife Federation.
    p. cm. — (Ranger Rick's naturescope)
    Originally published: New York: Learning Triangle Press, c 1998.
    Includes bibliographical references and index.
    ISBN 0-7910-4878-0 (pt. 1) — ISBN 0-7910-4879-9 (pt. 2)
    1. Mammals—Study and teaching (Elementary)—Activity programs.
    I. National Wildlife Federation. II. Series.
    [Ql706.4.A535 1998]
    372.3'57—dc21   98-39958
                                                         CIP

NatureScope® was originally conceived by National Wildlife Federation's School Programs Editorial Staff, under the direction of Judy Braus, Editor. Special thanks to all of the Editorial Staff, Scientific, Educational Consultants and Contributors who brought this series of eighteen publications to life.

TM and ® designate trademarks of National Wildlife Federation and are used, under license, by The McGraw-Hill Companies, Inc. and Chelsea House.

Other Titles in Ranger Rick's NatureScope

AMAZING MAMMALS, PART I
AMAZING MAMMALS, PART II
ASTRONOMY ADVENTURES
BIRDS, BIRDS, BIRDS
DIGGING INTO DINOSAURS
DISCOVERING DESERTS
DIVING INTO OCEANS
GEOLOGY: THE ACTIVE EARTH
INCREDIBLE INSECTS

LETS HEAR IT FOR HERPS:
ALL ABOUT AMPHIBIANS AND REPTILES
POLLUTION: PROBLEMS & SOLUTIONS
RAIN FORESTS: TROPICAL TREASURES
TREES ARE TERRIFIC!
WADING INTO WETLANDS
WILD ABOUT WEATHER
WILD & CRAFTY

TABLE OF CONTENTS

A Close-Up Look At Amazing Mammals

ooking at the Table of Contents, you can see we've divided *Amazing Mammals—Part II* into eight chapters (each of which deals with specific kinds of mammals). Each of the eight chapters includes *background information* that explains concepts and vocabulary, *activities* that relate to the chapter theme, and *Copycat Pages* that reinforce many of the concepts introduced in the activities.

You can choose single activity ideas or teach each chapter as a unit. Either way, each activity stands by itself and includes teaching objectives, a list of materials needed, suggested age groups, subjects covered, and a step-by-step explanation of how to do the activity. (The objectives, materials, age groups, and subjects are highlighted in the left-hand margin for easy reference.)

AGE GROUPS

The suggested age groups are:

- Primary (grades K-2)
- Intermediate (grades 3-5)
- Advanced (grades 6-8)

Each chapter begins with primary activities and ends with intermediate or advanced activities. But don't feel bound by the grade levels we suggest. You'll be able to adapt many of the activities to fit your particular age group and needs.

OUTDOOR ACTIVITIES

No matter where you live there are many mammal-related activities you can do outside. We've included several outdoor activities in this issue. These are coded in the chapters in which they appear with this symbol:

COPYCAT PAGES

The *Copycat Pages* supplement the activities and include ready-to-copy games, puzzles, coloring pages, and worksheets. *Answers to all Copycat Pages are in the texts of the activities.*

WHAT'S AT THE END

Applying Your Knowledge and the Bibliography are loaded with reference suggestions that include books, films, and mammal posters. It also has mammal questions and answers, a mammal glossary, and suggestions for where to get more mammal information.

PUTTING ORDER TO THE MAMMALS

As we mentioned in *Amazing Mammals—Part I*, not all mammalogists agree on how many mammalian orders there are or about which mammals fit where. In this issue we focus on many of the major mammal groups and some of the smaller ones, combining several mammal orders in certain chapters. We didn't base the order of the chapters on taxonomy or evolutionary history.

THE PRIMATES

O n the island of Madagascar there's a rare, strange-looking little mammal called the aye-aye (EYE-eye). With its big, bushy tail and slender body, the aye-aye looks a little like an oversized squirrel. It builds large, leafy nests in the trees, and it gnaws on wood with its rodentlike front teeth.

But despite its appearance and habits, the aye-aye isn't related to squirrels—or to any other rodent, for that matter. It's related, in fact, to humans—and to the baboons, chimpanzees, orangutans, and others that, along with the aye-aye, make up the group of mammals known as the *primates*.

aye-aye

A PRIMATE PRIMER

Just what *is* a primate? It's difficult to give a quick and easy definition, since there's so much variation among the different species. (Compare an aye-aye, for example, with a human.) But all primates have several or all of the following characteristics:

The Gift of Grasp: Being able to grasp objects with fingers and/or toes is a typical primate "talent." (Some other mammals, such as rodents, have the ability to grasp, but not nearly to the extent that primates do.) Since most primates spend a lot of their time in trees (some, in fact, rarely come down to the ground), a knack for holding onto branches and vines really comes in handy.

Thumbs Up for Thumbs: Another primate specialty is an *opposable thumb*—a thumb that can rotate in such a way that its tip touches the tips of the fingers. Opposable thumbs increase primates' manual dexterity. (Opossums and a few other non-primates also have opposable thumbs, but their hands aren't nearly so dextrous as those of primates.)

A few primates—those, for example, that spend a lot of time swinging arm over arm through the trees—lack opposable thumbs or have only very small or semi-opposable thumbs. (A well-developed opposable thumb would get in their way and slow down their travel.) Gorillas and some other primates, though, have opposable "thumbs" (big toes) on their feet as well as on their hands.

Getting in Touch: Primate hands and feet are special in another way too. Over the years, the tips of their fingers and toes have evolved into very sensitive organs of touch. Claws, which grow out of the ends of many mammals' digits, have gradually become fingernails and toenails on the *backs* of primates' digits, leaving more space on finger and toe tips for touching.

The Brainy Bunch: Mammals, in general, are a pretty intelligent group. (For more about how mammals' brains compare with those of other animals, see "The Layered Wolf" on page 12 of *NatureScope: Amazing Mammals—Part I.*) And many of the primates are among the best "thinkers" in the bunch. Their brains are larger in relation to their body sizes than those of most other animals, and as a group they probably have a higher capacity for learning than any other animal group does. (Some scientists, though, think that dolphins and other whales may rival the primates when it comes to brain power.)

Seeing in Stereo: People and most other primates make a poor showing when their sense of smell is compared with that of other mammals. But when it comes to eyesight, they rank far above the others. They can see color—an unusual ability among the mammals—and their eyes face forward so that the view each of their eyes perceives overlaps with that of the other eye. This overlapping eyesight, called *stereoscopic vision,* helps primates judge distances. (Most mammal carnivores also have forward-facing eyes and stereoscopic vision. But almost all other mammals have eyes located on the sides of their heads.)

Group Dynamics: Although a few kinds of primates are loners, most spend their entire lives as part of a group. Group living has a lot of advantages, but one of its main pluses is the concept of safety in numbers. (For more about this concept, see page 26.)

There's usually a lot of cooperation and interaction among the members of a primate social group. For example, most primates take turns *grooming* each other: looking through each other's fur and removing dirt, ticks, and other "riffraff." This not only helps members of the group stay healthy, but it also helps establish and maintain bonds within the group.

WHO'S WHO AMONG THE PRIMATES

When we hear the word *primate,* most of us probably think of gorillas or chimps—or maybe even ourselves. These primates belong to the *anthropoids,* one of two main primate groups. (*Anthropoid* means "resembling man.") The other main group of primates, called the *prosimians,* is a lot less humanlike than the anthropoids. Here's a look at both primate groups and at some of the representatives of each:

An Overview of the Anthropoids: Humans, apes, and monkeys all belong to the anthropoid primate group. Except for humans, who have adapted to living in almost every habitat and climate in the world, most anthropoids are confined to tropical or subtropical areas. Many, such as orangutans and spider monkeys, stick to the forests—but a few, such as baboons, live on the open savannah.

A lot of people use the words *monkey* and *ape* interchangeably, but these words

4　　gorilla　　　　　　　　　　gibbon　　　　　　　　　　　　　　　　proboscis monkey

actually refer to two different kinds of animals. The main differences between these mammals have to do with the structure of the skeleton (especially the skull). But you can usually tell a monkey from an ape by the fact that most monkeys have tails. Also, most monkeys probably aren't so intelligent as the apes are.

Baboons, colobus monkeys, macaques, marmosets, and tamarins are all examples of monkeys. Chimpanzees, gibbons, gorillas, and orangutans, on the other hand, are all types of apes.

Prosimians—the "Primitive" Ones: Scientists think that the earliest primates were probably very similar to some of the animals that belong to this group. Some prosimians have longer, more doglike snouts than anthropoids do, and their sense of smell is more highly developed. They tend to be smaller than the anthropoids, and their brains aren't as large in relation to the size of their bodies. Most live in tropical forests in Africa (including the island of Madagascar) or Asia.

The aye-aye mentioned in the introduction to this chapter is a prosimian. So are bush babies, lemurs, lorises, pottos, and tarsiers. As different from humans as these mammals look, we all have a lot in common. And we share an ancestry that goes back at least 70 million years.

LOOKING AHEAD

Unfortunately, the future for many primate species is not very secure. The main problem primates face is one that's affecting many kinds of animals these days: large-scale destruction of habitat. Most primates live in the tropics—areas that are changing fast as human populations continue to explode and as unwise exploitation of resources increases.

For some primates, such as gorillas, poaching is another big problem. Poachers kill these animals not only for their meat, but also for their skins, skulls, and hands. The meat often ends up in restaurants in nearby towns, and the skins, skulls, and hands become tourists' souvenirs. (Gorilla hands are often fashioned into ashtrays.)

But the outlook for primates isn't hopeless. In fact, a lot of progress has been made toward ensuring their survival. Conservation organizations are working to protect habitats, control poaching, and educate people about primates. And zoos and research centers are cooperating with other organizations and with governments in developing breeding and reintroduction programs. Getting involved with the efforts of these organizations is one way you can help solve the problems primates face. (See "Hope for the Future" on page 55 of *NatureScope: Amazing Mammals—Part I* for the names of some organizations you can support.)

orangutan   red colobus monkey   baboon

Thumbless Relay

Run a thumbless relay race.

Objectives:
Describe what an opposable thumb is. Talk about some of the ways opposable thumbs are useful to people and other primates.

Ages:
Primary and Intermediate

Materials:
- *wide masking tape*
- *yarn or string*

Subject:
Science

What would life be like without opposable thumbs? Your kids can find out by running a special kind of relay race. Before you begin the race, talk about opposable thumbs using the background information on page 3. To help the kids visualize just what an opposable thumb is, have them touch one of their thumbs to the tip of each finger on the same hand. Then explain that this ability to swing the thumb across the hand helps people and the other primates who have an opposable thumb perform a lot of tasks that would otherwise be very difficult—or even impossible. Ask the kids if they can think of some things they do every day that would be a lot harder without opposable thumbs. (getting dressed, writing, holding onto eating utensils, playing certain sports, and so on)

Next point out that, like people, other primates also use their opposable thumbs in specific ways. Thumbs are a big help, for example, during grooming sessions. Without them, many apes and monkeys would have a hard time picking dirt, insects, and ticks out of each other's hair.

After your discussion, tell the kids that they're going to get to see for themselves just how useful opposable thumbs are. To do this, they'll need to become "thumbless" for awhile. Tape the kids' thumbs to their palms with wide masking tape—or, if you're working with older kids, have them work in small groups to tape each other's

thumbs. (Make sure the thumbs are securely taped and can't work their way out. The "tapers" may need to run the tape completely around the kids' hands a couple of times.) Then divide the group into two teams, give each team a two-foot (60-cm) piece of yarn or string, and take everyone outside.

Set up your relay lines so that they're about 50 feet (15 m) from a fence, a bike rack, a tree with low branches, or some other object that the kids can reach. Explain that each team member, in turn, will have to run up to the object and tie the piece of yarn or string to it. (You can have the kids tie either simple half knots [half hitches] or bows, depending on their ages and skill levels.) Then the team member must untie the yarn or string and bring it back to the next person in line. The winner of the relay is the first team whose members all successfully tie and untie the yarn.

After the race, carefully remove the tape from the kids' hands. Talk about what it was like to be thumbless. Then have the kids speculate about what might have happened if people had never evolved the adaptation we call opposable thumbs. Do they think the world would be just the same as it is today? Would people have been able to develop aspects of culture such as written language, art, music, and technology?

Of course, these questions can't really be answered with any certainty. Point out that the human brain is the main factor responsible for the way our cultures and societies have developed. Also bring up the possibility that if people hadn't developed opposable thumbs, some other adaptation might have evolved that could have served a similar function. For example, point out that spider monkeys don't have thumbs at all. But the undersides of the ends of their tails are equipped with a super-sensitive, fleshy pad. This pad helps them to grasp objects as big as a tree limb or as small as a piece of grass. Having such a dextrous tail seems to compensate for the spider monkey's lack of a thumb.

male chacma baboon

Leonard Lee Rue III

Face It!

Objectives:
Discuss the importance of primate facial expressions. Name some ways other animals express "moods" or convey messages about themselves. Describe several facial expressions of chimpanzees and talk about how chimps use these expressions.

Ages:
Intermediate

Materials:
- *copies of page 11*
- *slips of paper*
- *pen or pencil*
- *chalkboard or easel paper*

Subject:
Science

- **aggression**
- **anger**
- **boredom**
- **confusion**
- **disbelief**
- **disgust**
- **embarrassment**
- **fear**
- **frustration**
- **impatience**
- **joy**
- **nervousness**
- **pain**
- **sadness**
- **surprise**

Most animals have the ability to communicate—and primates are among the greatest communicators of all. To help your kids learn about some of the ways primates communicate, try this activity.

Start by writing each of the words in the margin on a separate slip of paper. Put the slips in a sack or other container. (The kids will be using them a little later.) Then write the words again on a chalkboard or large piece of easel paper.

Next talk about some of the ways animals communicate and express messages about themselves. Explain that many primates can convey a wide variety of information to each other using facial expressions. Most other animals don't rely on facial expressions as heavily as primates do. The muscles in their faces aren't as "finely tuned" as those of primates, so their range of expressions is much more limited. But they often have other means of expressing themselves. Ask the kids if they can think of any examples. (A dog

Luise Woelflein

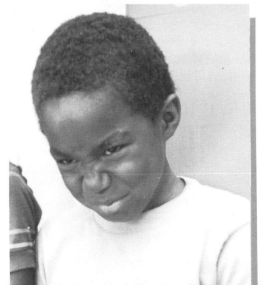

may bark if it wants to go outside, a cat may purr when it's content, and so on.)

Now ask the kids to describe some facial expressions that we—the primates known as people—often use. (We smile when we're happy or amused, raise our eyebrows when we're surprised, grimace when we taste something sour, and so on.) Explain that people have the most complex and sophisticated repertoire of expressions among the primates. But other primates, such as chimpanzees, also communicate and express themselves with a wide range of facial expressions.

To show how effective facial expressions can be in communicating attitudes, emotions, moods, and so on, have a different volunteer act out each of the words you listed earlier. Let each performer pick one of the words from the sack. Explain that the volunteers must use facial expressions to portray the word. They can also use appropriate sounds if they want to—but they aren't allowed to say words. As each volunteer acts out his or her word, have the rest of the kids try to identify which emotion or attitude the volunteer is communicating. They can narrow down their choices by referring to the list you wrote on the board.

After you've gone through all of the words listed, pass out copies of page 11. Explain that chimpanzees use a wide range of facial expressions to communicate certain messages and to express certain emotions. Chimps are also very vocal animals, and they emit particular sounds, such as whimpers, hoots, or squeals, with most of the characteristic faces they display. (All but face #2 on page 11 are usually accompanied by sounds.) Can the kids think of some typical sounds humans make that go along with certain facial expressions? (Laughter often accompanies a grin, a gasp may go along with a surprised look, screaming sometimes accompanies an expression of fear, and so on.)

Now use the following information to go over each of the chimp faces. The words in italics are the names scientists have given to the expressions.

(continued next page)

1. Like several of the faces pictured on the page, this *open grin* has a couple of different meanings. Chimps who are either very excited or very frightened display this expression. For example, chimps who find a big supply of a favorite food may "grin" and scream loudly. So will a chimp that's being attacked by another chimp or by a predator.

2. When a chimp compresses its lips and the hair around its face bristles, the animal is not in a friendly mood! A chimp that's attacking an enemy or is otherwise showing aggressive behavior adopts this expression. Ask the kids if they've ever seen a person (such as a parent!) tighten up his or her lips in anger.

3. This *pout* often means that a chimp wants something from another chimp. For example, a chimp may whimper softly and wear this expression when it wants another chimp to groom it or share food with it. Chimps who are frustrated for one reason or another may also pout and whimper. Ask the kids if this behavior sounds familiar!

4. During play, chimps wear this *play face*. They also make characteristic grunting sounds that researchers have described as laughter.

5. A chimp who has just been attacked by a more dominant member of its group often shows this expression, called a *horizontal pout*. (Chimp societies are made up of as many as 50 individuals, and each animal has a social rank.)

The horizontal pout is a signal of submission, and it's often accompanied by whimpering sounds.

6. Like the open grin shown in the first picture, this *closed grin* often means that a chimp is either excited or frightened. But the excitement or fear is less intense than that shown in the open grin. Chimps often make squeaking sounds when they grin in this way.

The closed grin also serves as a way of appeasing superior chimps: Lower-ranking chimps often use it when approaching a more dominant animal. In one of her books about chimpanzees, entitled *In the Shadow of Man*, Jane Goodall wrote, "If the human nervous or social smile has its equivalent expression in the chimpanzee it is, without doubt, the closed grin."

Junior Editors

Read a short story about gorillas and find out what's wrong with it.

Objectives:
Identify some inaccurate information about gorillas. Explain why accuracy in journalism is important. Discuss some misconceptions concerning other mammals.

Ages:
Advanced

Materials:
- ***copies of pages 12 and 13***
- ***reference books***

Subjects:
Science and Journalism

 gigantic, raging ape fills the movie screen. Having plundered his way through the streets of New York City, killing people and destroying buildings along the way, he's now making his last stand on top of the Empire State Building. A fleet of dwarfed, gun-equipped airplanes buzz through the air, trying to kill the violent beast and rescue the delicate woman he has kidnapped.

Sound familiar? That vicious brute—a giant Hollywood gorilla named King Kong—made movie history when the original film by the same name hit the theaters in 1933. His behavior was typical of the savage image people had attributed to gorillas for years. But that image and the misconceptions that go along with it have since been proven wrong. Within the last 30 years gorilla researchers have discovered that these large primates are unaggressive, elusive animals. When danger threatens, they usually try to escape by running away—even though they're very strong and powerful.

Here's an activity that will help your kids learn about gorillas by identifying some incorrect information about them. It'll also get them thinking about some common misconceptions about other mammals.

Begin by telling the kids to pretend that they're editors of a science and nature magazine. Have them imagine that they receive many articles and stories each week from different writers. Part of their jobs as editors is to decide which of the articles and stories should be printed in their magazine.

Ask the "editors" what kinds of requirements they think an article or story must meet in order to make it into their magazine. Explain that because different magazines have different themes (e.g., science, sports, food, or whatever), they all have different requirements. But all good magazines look for stories and articles that are well-written, interesting, and technically accurate. To find out whether or not a story or an article is accurate, editors often do research on whatever the piece is about. This may involve, among other things, digging into reference books and looking up articles on the subject.

Next ask the kids why it's so important

for editors to make sure that the information in a piece is accurate. Point out that even the best publications make mistakes, but if a publication makes too many of them, its reputation can be damaged. And wrong information can lead to or perpetuate misconceptions about a subject. Sometimes these misconceptions can give the subject a bad image. (For example, misinterpreted, inaccurate, and sometimes even completely fabricated accounts of gorilla behavior gave these primates a reputation they didn't deserve.) Even if wrong information isn't particularly damaging to a subject (calling a gorilla a monkey, for example, when it's really an ape), it still contributes to a general misunderstanding of it.

Now pass out a copy of page 12 to each person and explain that the story on the page represents an excerpt from a story that they—the editors—recently received from an author. Explain that they need to check out the accuracy of the piece to decide whether or not it should be printed in their magazine. Then give the kids research time to discover the problems with it. Tell them to underline any words or phrases that they think are inaccurate. They should number each word or phrase

they underline, then write the reason it's wrong on the backs of their sheets.

Depending on the skill level of your group, you might want to tell the kids to keep the following things in mind while they're doing their research:
- area of the world where gorillas live
- habitat
- behavior
- food preferences and feeding habits
- physical features

When everyone's finished, go over the story and the wrong information it contains. We've printed the piece below and italicized the inaccuracies. Each italicized phrase is numbered, and each number corresponds to an explanation of why the phrase is wrong. (See "What's Wrong with the Gorilla Story?" on page 10.)

If you're working with older kids, ask them if any of the information in the story is accurate. (Gorillas do live in groups. A group's leader is usually an adult male, and he decides what the group will do and where it will travel. Another thing that's correct is the fact that gorillas do eat leaves and fruit, as well as other vegetation.) Finally, have them rewrite the piece to make it completely accurate.

As the sun's first rays brightened the forest, a *group of more than sixty gorillas*[1] climbed out of their *treetop nests*.[2] They *chattered and screeched noisily*[3] as they *traveled arm over arm among the branches*.[4] Throwing their *long tails*[5] out behind them for balance, they made their way down to the ground. There they waited for their leader—an adult male gorilla with a *light brown back*[6]—to decide which direction they'd travel in.

Weighing only *650 pounds (293 kg), the gorilla leader was smaller than most males his age*.[7] But he was strong and *very ferocious, even for a gorilla*.[8] He looked around at his group, then turned and moved toward the tall grasses of the *South American savannah*.[9] The other *monkeys*[10] followed, feeding on leaves and fruits as they went.

Most of the group stayed together, traveling in typical gorilla fashion: on the *palms of their hands*[11] and the soles of their feet. But two of the females lagged behind the rest of the group. Both were *carrying year-old babies in their arms*,[12] so they were forced to *walk slowly along on their hind legs*.[13]

Suddenly the leader stopped moving. The others did the same. Their *keen noses*[14] had caught the scent of a *herd of antelopes—a favorite gorilla food*.[15] The leader rose up on his hind legs to try to catch sight of the herd. But *gorilla eyesight is weak*,[16] and the herd was still out of sight. *The gorillas would have to follow their noses for awhile*.[17]

WHAT'S WRONG WITH THE GORILLA STORY?

1. Gorillas live in groups of from two to thirty animals.
2. Gorillas build their sleeping nests either on the ground or in a tree's lower branches. (Gorillas are too heavy to risk sleeping high up in the treetops.)
3. Gorillas usually aren't very vocal and are usually quiet as they they travel through their habitats. Many monkeys, on the other hand, do make a lot of noise.
4. Traveling arm over arm through the treetops, called *brachiation*, is not a common mode of travel for gorillas. They aren't adapted for moving long distances through the trees, and they spend a lot more time on the ground than many other primates do.
5. Gorillas, like all apes, don't have tails.
6. Adult male gorillas have a saddle of silver (not light brown) hair on their backs.
7. Most gorillas weigh between 150 and 400 pounds (68 and 180 kg). And the leader of the group is often one of the largest males.
8. Despite their reputations as being fierce and nasty, gorillas are relatively peaceful and unaggressive.
9. Gorillas live in Africa, not South America, and their habitat is rain forest rather than savannah.
10. Gorillas aren't monkeys—they're apes. (For an explanation of the difference between the two, see page 5.)
11. Gorillas usually walk so that the weight of their hindquarters falls on the soles of their feet, while the weight of their forequarters falls on the *knuckles*—not the palms—of their hands.
12. Gorilla mothers often hold infant gorillas in their arms, just as human mothers do. But by the time a young gorilla is about four months old, it rides on its mother's back.
13. Gorillas *are* capable of walking on two legs—but only for short distances.
14. Like all primates, gorillas have a relatively weak sense of smell.
15. Gorillas don't hunt antelopes. Although captive gorillas will eat some meat, wild gorillas seem to stick to fruits, bark, shoots, and other vegetation.
16. Gorilla eyesight—like that of all primates—is good. It ranks far above the eyesight of most other mammals.
17. See number 14.

BRANCHING OUT: OTHER MAMMAL MISCONCEPTIONS

Now that your kids have learned some facts and fallacies about gorillas, have them discover the truth behind some other mammal misconceptions. Pass out copies of page 13 and give the kids research time to figure out whether each statement is true or false. For each statement they think is false, have them write why they think it's false and what the truth is. Here are the answers:

1. *Raccoons wash their food.* False. This idea came from the fact that captive raccoons often dunk their food in their water dishes. But they aren't really washing their food. They're just instinctively going through the motions of "finding" their food in water as wild raccoons do.
2. *Bats are blind.* False. All bats can see—and a few even have better vision than people do! Most, though, don't have an exceptionally keen sense of sight. They rely on their ability to echolocate to help them navigate. (See page 34 for more about bats and echolocation.)
3. *Camels store water in their humps.* False. Camels' humps contain fat—an energy reserve that helps these desert animals survive when food and water supplies run low. As camels use up the fat they've stored, their humps get soft and flabby.
4. *Bulls get angry when they see red.* False. Like most mammals, bulls are color-blind. They often react strongly to movement, though. When a bull charges toward a matador's red cape during a bullfight, it's reacting to the cape's waving motion—not its color.
5. *Porcupines shoot their quills.* False. A porcupine can't take aim and hurl its quills at an attacker, but it can raise them as a threat. The quills are loosely attached to the porcupine's skin, and they come out very easily when their pointed ends stick into another animal.
6. *Chimpanzees are vegetarians.* False. Chimps do eat a lot of fruits, leaves, bark, and other vegetation—and for years many people thought that's pretty much all they ate. But in the 1960s chimp researchers discovered that they sometimes kill and eat animals such as young wild pigs and baboons.

1. Chimp is very excited or frightened.

2. Chimp is aggressive.

3. Chimp wants something or is frustrated.

4. Chimp is playful.

5. Chimp has just been attacked or is otherwise being submissive.

6. Chimp is moderately excited or frightened.

As the sun's first rays brightened the forest, a group of more than sixty gorillas climbed out of their treetop nests. They chattered and screeched noisily as they traveled arm over arm among the branches. Throwing their long tails out behind them for balance, they made their way down to the ground. There they waited for their leader—an adult male gorilla with a light brown back—to decide which direction they'd travel in.

Weighing only 650 pounds (293 kg), the gorilla leader was smaller than most males his age. But he was strong and very ferocious, even for a gorilla. He looked around at his group, then turned and moved toward the tall grasses of the South American savannah. The other monkeys followed, feeding on leaves and fruits as they went.

Most of the group stayed together, traveling in typical gorilla fashion: on the palms of their hands and the soles of their feet. But two of the females lagged behind the rest of the group. Both were carrying year-old babies in their arms, so they were forced to walk slowly along on their hind legs.

Suddenly the leader stopped moving. The others did the same. Their keen noses had caught the scent of a herd of antelopes—a favorite gorilla food. The leader rose up on his hind legs to try to catch sight of the herd. But gorilla eyesight is weak, and the herd was still out of sight. The gorillas would have to follow their noses for awhile.

True _____
False _____

1. Raccoons wash their food.

True _____
False _____

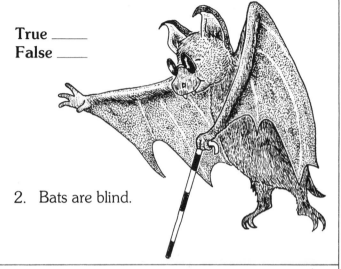

2. Bats are blind.

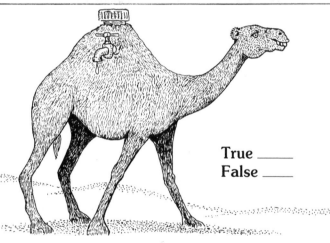

True _____
False _____

3. Camels store water in their humps.

True _____
False _____

4. Bulls get angry when they see red.

True _____
False _____

5. Porcupines shoot their quills.

6. Chimpanzees are vegetarians.

True _____
False _____

THE CARNIVORES

If you've ever watched a cat stalking a bird or a dog chasing a squirrel, you've seen a carnivore in action. In this chapter we'll take a look at the characteristics shared by cats, dogs, bears, raccoons, weasels, civets, hyenas, and other carnivores, and see how members of this group differ from one another.

CARNIVORE CHARACTERISTICS

Meaty Meals: Carnivores eat meat. Many hunt and kill their own prey; others rely on carrion as their main source of meat. Although all of the mammals in this group are descended from strict meat eaters, some are omnivorous, and a few feed almost entirely on plants. For example, raccoons eat everything from crayfish to persimmons, and giant pandas eat mainly bamboo roots and shoots. (For more about carnivores, omnivores, and herbivores, see "Finding Food" on pages 35-36 of *NatureScope: Amazing Mammals—Part I.*)

"The Better to Eat You With ...": One thing all carnivores have in common is a mix of specialized teeth. For example, most carnivores have long, pointed canines that they use to stab and kill their prey. And unlike all other mammals, they have *carnassial* teeth. Carnassials are sharp cheek teeth that cut like scissors when the animal closes its jaws. Cats, wolves, and other carnivores that are fairly strict meat eaters have very sharp carnassials. But carnivores that have omnivorous diets, such as bears and raccoons, tend to have flatter, less scissorlike carnassials. (These omnivores also tend to have larger rear molars, which help grind their food.)

Paws with Claws: Almost all carnivores have claws, but they use their claws in different ways. They may use them to hold their prey, dig for food, dig dens or burrows, climb trees, and so on. Most cats and some other carnivores have sharp, *retractile* claws. That means they can be sheathed, or pulled back. When the claws are sheathed, a special ligament holds each claw and the toe bone it's attached to out of the way. But when the animal needs to use its claws, muscles straighten out the toe bones and unsheathe the claws. Many other carnivores, such as wolves, have *nonretractile* claws, which cannot be sheathed. And a few carnivores, such as cheetahs, have claws that are *partially retractile.*

Sensing It!: Smell is one of the most important and well-developed senses in carnivores. These mammals use their powerful noses to detect

RETRACTILE CLAWS

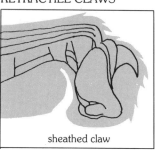

sheathed claw

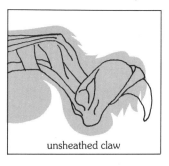

unsheathed claw

CAT SKULL

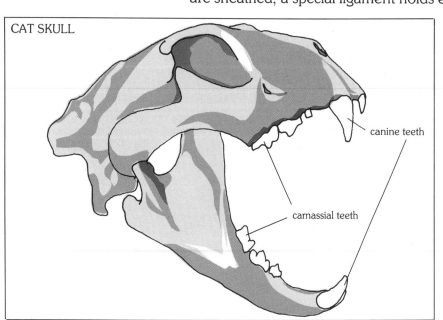

canine teeth

carnassial teeth

prey. They also communicate with each other by producing special scents. (Different scents help them recognize territorial boundaries, identify individuals, and identify females that are ready to mate.) Some carnivores have a sense of smell that is a hundred times more sensitive than that of humans.

Smell isn't the only sense that's well developed in carnivores. Most also have keen hearing and sharp eyesight. All carnivores have eyes that face forward, giving them good depth perception. And many have eyes that are adapted to seeing well in the dark.

GROWING UP A CARNIVORE

Family Life: Carnivores tend to spend a lot more time raising and caring for their young than many other mammals do. For example, female polar bears may keep their young with them for more than two years. This extended care period gives the young time to learn how to survive.

Games to Grow By: When young carnivores play, they may be "having a good time." But as they pounce, tumble, and run they are also developing their coordination, strengthening their muscles, and learning hunting skills. And they also may be learning the social rules of their species and their rank in the social order.

As they get older, young carnivores sharpen their hunting skills. Some female carnivores, such as cheetahs, may bring home wounded prey and release it for the young to catch. And many young carnivores go along on hunts to watch and learn how the hunting is done.

THE HUNTING LIFE

Hunting Strategies: Carnivores have many different methods of catching their prey. Some carnivores, such as most cats, hunt alone, stalking their prey or waiting for it in ambush. But others may hunt in pairs (foxes) or in larger groups (wolves). By hunting in a group, some carnivores can overcome prey animals much larger than themselves.

Slap, Grab, and Stab: Each carnivore species has a characteristic way of killing its prey. Most kill by biting the prey—either in the neck (lions), on the back of the head (weasels), or in a soft spot, such as the abdomen (African hunting dogs). Some use their paws and claws to knock down their prey first and to hold onto it as they bite (cats), but others don't use their paws or claws at all—they just grab the prey with their teeth (African hunting dogs).

Easy Pickin's: Whether they're ambushing zebras on an African plain or stalking mice in a field, carnivores help regulate the populations of the animals that they feed on. Since most healthy adult prey can usually outrun predators, successfully hide from them, or use their antlers, horns, hooves or other weapons to escape unharmed, carnivores usually catch the young, old, injured, or sick animals.

Sea Otter Picture Books

What carnivore eats one-fourth its body weight in shellfish and fish every day, spends most of its life in the ocean, and played a role in opening up the American West? The sea otter! By making their own sea otter picture books, the kids in your group will learn all about these mammals.

Start by asking the kids what carnivores are and if they know any examples of mammals that are carnivores. (Use the background information on pages 14-15 in your discussion.) Then ask the kids how they feel about carnivores. Do any of the kids think carnivores are mean because they eat other animals? (To help the kids understand that carnivores aren't mean, you might want to play the song "I'm Just Hungry" from Bill Brennan's album, *When My Shoes Are Loose* [Do Dreams Music, P.O. Box 5623, Takoma Park, MD 20913].)

Now show the kids a picture of a sea otter. Explain that these carnivores spend most of their lives in the ocean. They are born at sea, hunt for food in the sea, and even sleep there. Then tell the kids that they're going to find out how these mammals survive in the sea. But first they must make their own sea otter picture books (see directions at the end of this activity).

When the kids have finished making their books, use the information below to talk about the pictures. Have the kids follow along in their books as you discuss each picture. You might want to show the kids other pictures of sea otters during your discussion. (As you go through the pages, have the kids write one or two words underneath each picture to help them remember facts about the sea otter. For example, they could write "kelp" under picture #1, "food" under picture #2, and so on.) Afterward, encourage the kids to draw their own pictures opposite the pictures they glued down. For example, across from picture #1 they could draw a picture of a sea otter "tied up" in the kelp, or opposite picture #3 they could draw a sea otter using a rock.

FACTS ABOUT SEA OTTERS

1. **Kelp**—Sea otters live along parts of the rocky coast of western North America and in a few coastal areas of the Soviet Union and Japan. They often live in kelp beds and feed on animals that live in these kelp "forests." Sea otters often wrap kelp around their bodies when they want to take a nap. (This keeps them from drifting away.) A mother sea otter may "buckle up" her pup in kelp, too, if she needs to leave it alone at the surface.

2. **Food**—Sea otters feed on all kinds of shellfish and other invertebrates including abalone, sea urchins, clams, and crabs. The sea otters pick these animals off the ocean bottom or kelp stalks, or dig them out of the mud or sand. Then they bring them to the surface to eat. Some sea otters also catch fish.

3. **Tools**—Sea otters are the only mammals other than primates that are known to use a tool for collecting food. To dislodge an abalone, the animal will bang a rock against the edge of the abalone shell. A sea otter will also carry a rock to the surface, lie on its back with the rock on its belly, and smash clams and other shellfish against the rock so it can get at the meat inside.

4. **Fur**—The ocean can get pretty cold, but sea otters have thick fur coats to keep them warm. In fact, they have about the densest fur of any mammal. (Sea otters were once hunted, almost to extinction, for these fur coats. This fur trade helped open up the American West by luring trappers and traders to hunt sea otters.) To keep their coats "working" right, sea otters must keep them clean. So they

lick their coats and carefully comb their fur with their paws.

5. **Keeping Clean**—After a meal, sea otters often roll around in the water to clean off. And sometimes there are gulls in the water nearby, waiting to snatch up any left-overs that come off the sea otter's bodies.

6. **Teeth**—Like many other carnivores, sea otters have teeth specialized for eating meat. But unlike some of these carnivores, sea otters don't have very sharp carnassial teeth. Instead, their cheek teeth are rounded—all the better for crushing shellfish!

7. **Whiskers**—Sea otters have fairly good underwater vision, but they rely mostly on touch to find their prey. Their whiskers are very sensitive feelers.

8. **Front Paws**—Sea otters use their front paws to feel and dig for food, to grab onto prey, to smash prey against a rock, and to eat. Their paws have pads on them that help protect them from the sharp spines and shells of their prey.

9. **Growing Up**—Mother sea otters take very good care of their young. They carefully groom their pups' fur, carry their pups around on their bellies, and teach them how to swim and find food.

10. **Predators**—Sea otters have very few natural enemies. In Alaska, bald eagles sometimes prey on sea otter pups. And great white sharks sometimes kill sea otters as well.

construction paper

Sea Otters

ple

KELP

HOW TO MAKE A PICTURE BOOK

Before you get started, cut the drawing paper in half across its width. Then pass out crayons or markers, glue, a pair of scissors, a copy of page 22, and ten sheets of the paper to each person. Now have the kids follow these directions to make their picture books:

1. Color the pictures on page 22.
2. Cut out the pictures *along the solid lines only.* (Don't cut off the numbers in the pictures.)
3. Glue each picture to a separate piece of paper and let dry. (The kids will be putting the pages together to form a book, so be sure they leave at least 1 inch [2.5 cm] of white space on the left-hand side of each sheet.)
4. After the pictures have dried completely, lay the picture pages on top of each other in order. (Put #1 at the top.)
5. Fold a piece of construction paper in half and lay the picture pages inside. Staple the construction paper and picture pages together along the fold (see diagram).

Cats of Many Colors

Identify some different cats, then make an accordion-style cat cut-out.

Objectives:
*Define camouflage.
Describe how camouflage helps some cats survive.*

Ages:
Intermediate

Materials:
- *copies of page 23*
- *copies of poems below*
- *scissors*
- *crayons or markers*
- *reference books*
- *chalkboard or easel paper*
- *pictures of different wild cats*

Subjects:
Science and Art

In this activity the kids in your group will learn about camouflage in cats. Then they can match cats to cat poems, and make their own cat cut-outs.

Begin by explaining that many mammals are *camouflaged*. The colors and markings on their coats help them blend into the backgrounds of their habitats and make them less visible to their enemies or prey. Then use the information at the end of this activity to discuss camouflage among the cats. You might want to show the kids pictures of the different cats as you discuss them.

After your discussion, copy these names onto a chalkboard or large sheet of easel paper: leopard, lion, black panther (a type of leopard), tiger, cheetah, jaguar, cougar, and snow leopard. Then pass out copies of the poems below and explain that each poem matches one of the cats you listed. Tell the kids they should use reference books to identify the cat in each poem. Afterward, go over the answers with the kids (see end of this activity). Then pass out copies of page 23 and have them follow the instructions below to make cat cut-outs. (To make the horse cut-out, see "A Horse of a Different Color" on page 29.)

HOW TO MAKE A CAT CUT-OUT

1. Cut *along the straight, solid lines* in the middle and top of the page.
2. Fold the cat cut-out like an accordion along the dotted lines. You will be cutting along the lines of the "top" cat, so make sure that it faces outward (see diagram).
3. Cut the outline of the top cat *along the solid lines only*. Be sure to hold the layers together firmly so that they don't slip. (To make this easier for younger kids, have them cut around each cat

cut

cut

fold like an accordion

Cat Verses

1
I've got a strong body
And very large paws,
Teeth made for killing
And powerful jaws.
When it's time for a hunt
The females take charge,
And the prey they go after
Are usually large.

2
On padded tiptoes
I move without sound.
I can jump twenty feet
In only one bound.
I often go swimming
Or lie under a tree.
And the stripes on my back
Make me harder to see.

3
In dark Asian forests
I ambush my prey.
And my dark-colored coat
Doesn't give me away.

Like all other leopards
I have spots on my back
Though you can't always tell
'Cause my coat is so black.

4
I'm active at night
But may sleep through the day,
And my fur has dark spots
On a background of gray.
I eat all kinds of prey
Including goats called markhor,
But unlike other big cats
I'm unable to roar.

5
It's Latin America
Where I always roam.
The tropical forests
Are the place I call home.
My light-colored coat
Is all covered with spots.
And within my rosettes
There are even more dots.

separately and then fold it like an accordion.)

4. Unfold the paper and then color each cat to match one of the cats identified in the poems (lion, jaguar, snow leopard, black panther, and tiger). The order of the cats does not matter. Have the kids use reference books to make their markings accurate.

5. Write the name of each cat on the back of its picture and then copy its poem onto the back as well.

CAT CAMOUFLAGE

Cats, like many other predators, usually get within a certain distance of their prey before they pounce on it or chase after it. If they pounce or start their chase from too far away, chances are the prey will escape. Among the things cats rely on to help them get within striking distance of prey is camouflage. The markings on most cats' coats break up the outlines of their bodies. This makes it hard for prey to recognize the predators' shapes. And even though most mammalian prey are colorblind, the dark and light patterns of the predators' coats help them blend in with the plants and rocks around them.

The tiger's orange coat and black pattern is a good example of how markings help a predator "melt" into its background. The dark black stripes run at right angles to the outline of the tiger's body. This helps break up the tiger's outline and makes the tiger look like a part of the habitat where it lives (see diagram).

The colors and markings of other cats serve the same function as the tiger's stripes. For example, many spotted cats, such as leopards, live in wooded areas where the sunlight comes through the trees in a mottled pattern. The dark spots on these cats' light-colored coats mimic this light and dark pattern and hide them from prey. The spots also help break up the outlines of their bodies. Similarly, the pale-colored coat of a lion blends in perfectly with the plains where it lives. And when they're young, most cats have spotted coats that may help hide them from predators.

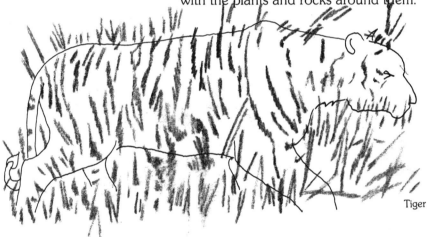

Tiger

Answers:
1—lion; 2—tiger; 3—black panther; 4—snow leopard; 5—jaguar

Clock a Carnivore

Observe a carnivore and record its behavior.

Objective:
Describe the behavior of a carnivore.

Ages:
Intermediate and Advanced

Materials:
● *chalkboard or easel paper*
(continued next page)

ave the kids in your group become "behavioral scientists" to learn about carnivore behavior. Before you get started, copy the "Carnivore Activities" listed at the end of the activity onto a chalkboard or large sheet of easel paper. Then start by reviewing the characteristics that make carnivores different from other kinds of mammals (see pages 14-15).

Next ask the kids if any of them have a pet carnivore (cat or dog). What kinds of activities have the kids noticed their pets or other neighborhood carnivores doing? (eating, playing, sleeping, and so on) As the kids list behaviors, write them on the chalkboard or easel paper. Then show the kids the list of activities you copied earlier. Combine the two lists by fitting as many of the kids' suggestions into the original list as you can. If the kids have any ideas that don't fit into one of the existing categories, add them to the list and give them a new letter code.

Now ask the kids what activity they think their pet carnivore does most of the

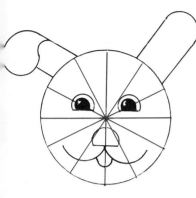

time. Write their ideas on the chalkboard or easel paper. Then tell them that they're going to test their ideas by using the list of coded activities to chart the behavior of a carnivore.

Draw this dog face onto the chalkboard or easel paper. Then pass out pencils and blank sheets of paper and have the kids copy it. (If they're going to clock a cat, have the kids change the face and ears so that it resembles a cat.) Also have them copy the list of carnivore activities onto the same sheet. Explain that the clock represents three hours and each of its divisions represents 15 minutes. Here's what they must do:

1. Find a time when your pet carnivore (or a neighborhood carnivore) is usually active and you have some time free for carnivore spying. Write the date and time you start watching at the top of your carnivore clock.

2. Watch your carnivore every fifteen minutes, for about two or three minutes, and write down the code for what the carnivore was doing each time you observed its behavior. For example, if your carnivore was *eating* the first time you watched it, write "E" in the first section of the clock. But if it took a *few* bites of food and then *groomed* itself for most of the time, write "G" on the clock.

3. For the next "round," write down the time of day, and then watch your carnivore again for about two or three minutes. Choose an activity code from the list and write it in the next space on

the clock. Keep doing this every fifteen minutes until you've filled up the clock. If your carnivore does something that's not on the list, add the behavior to the list and give it a new letter code.

Note: You might want to have the kids watch their pets for a continuous half hour, but this can become tedious—especially if the pet is sleeping most of the time. If you're at a nature center that has a raccoon or other wild carnivore, have the kids observe it instead of a pet.

Afterward have the kids bring in their carnivore clocks and talk about their data. Did each child's carnivore spend most of its time doing what he or she thought it would? Ask the kids if they think they can make any generalizations about the behavior of their carnivores after having clocked them for a few hours. Explain that scientists have to make a lot of observations before they can make generalizations about the behavior of wild animals. And they also have to watch more than one animal to generalize about the behavior of a particular species. If the kids really wanted to know what an animal does most of the time, or something else about its behavior, they'd have to observe it for many days, weeks, and months.

If you want, have the kids clock their carnivores for several days in a row. Afterward they can compare what they learned after several days of observation with what they learned after just three hours.

Carnivore Activities

C—Climbing

E—Eating

G—Grooming

H—Human contact (playing, getting petted)

B—Going to the bathroom

P—Chasing or catching prey

R—Running

S—Sleeping, sitting, staring

W—Walking around

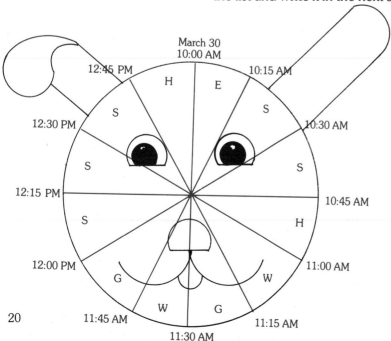

A Logic Game

Objectives:
Define digitigrade *and* plantigrade. *Describe the difference between* retractile *and* nonretractile *claws. Describe some characteristics of several carnivores.*

Ages:
Advanced

Materials:
- *copies of page 24*
- *chalkboard or easel paper (optional)*
- *pencils*

Subject:
Science

Here's a fun way to get the kids in your group thinking logically while teaching them some characteristics of several carnivores. Start by explaining that mammalogists divide mammals into different groups. One of these groups is the *carnivores*. Ask the kids to name some of the mammals that belong to the carnivore group. (lions, bears, wolves, raccoons, weasels, and so on) Then ask them what kinds of characteristics the carnivores have that set them apart from other kinds of mammals. (Use the information on pages 14-15 to talk about the characteristics of the carnivores.)

Next explain that some carnivores, such as bears, walk on flat feet, just as people do. These carnivores are called *plantigrade*. Other carnivores, such as cats, dogs, and wolves, walk on their toes and are called *digitigrade*.

Now tell the kids that they are going to get a chance to solve a carnivore mystery. Pass out copies of page 24 and tell the kids to read the scenario at the top of the page. Make sure they understand that they must figure out the identity of each of the seven mammals and that all the information they need is on the sheet.

If they're having trouble getting started, copy the chart below onto a chalkboard or large sheet of easel paper. But don't copy the animal names or the yes and no answers! Then, using the information given in the clue for animal #1, fill in the first column of the chart. Tell the kids to copy the chart and fill in as much of the rest of it as they can using the information for animals #2 to 7. Then have them list the information that "John remembers" in columns under their charts (see diagram below chart). By comparing the information in their charts with that in the columns, the kids should be able to figure out which animal is which. Then they can fill in all of the "missing" information in their charts. Afterward, go over the kids' answers using the answers shown in the chart.

To make the puzzle a little easier for younger kids, copy the completed chart shown here onto a chalkboard or large sheet of easel paper. Have them copy it and then use only the information that "John remembers" to figure out which carnivore on the chart is which.

COMPLETED CHART

	Polar Bear Animal #1	Bobcat Animal #2	Giant Panda Animal #3	River Otter Animal #4	Gray Fox Animal #5	Hyena Animal #6	Gray Wolf Animal #7
Is it native to North America?	Yes	Yes	No	Yes	Yes	No	Yes
Does it have retractile claws?	No	Yes	No	No	No	No	No
Does it spend most of its time on land?	No	Yes	Yes	No	Yes	Yes	Yes
Is it digitigrade?	No	Yes	No	Yes	Yes	Yes	Yes
Is it a strict meat eater?	Yes	Yes	No	Yes	No	Yes	Yes

"WHAT JOHN REMEMBERS"

Not Strict Meat Eaters	Strict Meat Eaters	Retractile Claws	Nonretractile Claws	Not Native to North America	Native to North America	Spends Most of Its Time away from Land	Spends Most of Its Time on Land	Plantigrade	Digitigrade
giant panda gray fox	polar bear river otter bobcat hyena gray wolf	bobcat	polar bear giant panda river otter hyena gray wolf gray fox	giant panda hyena	polar bear river otter bobcat gray fox gray wolf	polar bear river otter	bobcat hyena giant panda gray fox gray wolf	polar bear giant panda	bobcat hyena river otter gray fox gray wolf

7

8

10   bald eagle

5

gull

9

4

2

clam

sea urchin

abalone

crab

6

3

rock

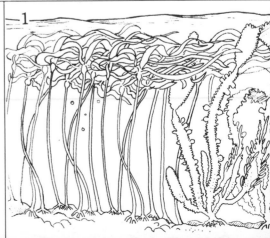

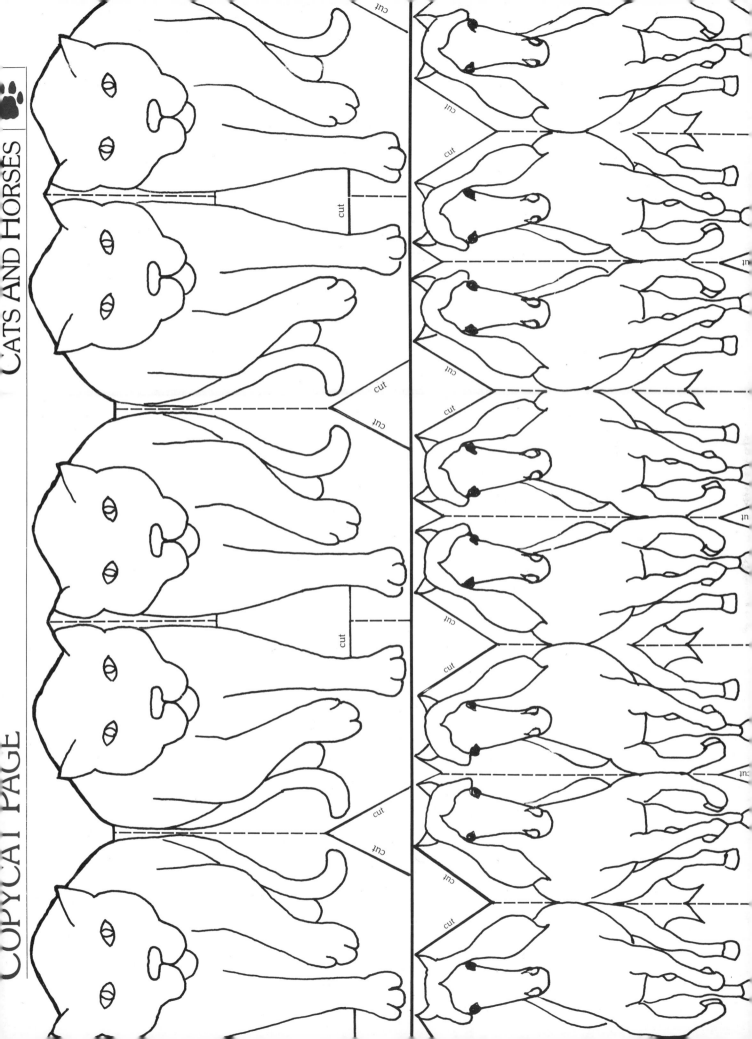

John Kempke was at the library doing some research for a school project on mammals. He had chosen to concentrate on these carnivores: polar bears, giant pandas, hyenas, gray wolves, bobcats, river otters, and gray foxes. And by reading through all kinds of books he found out lots of information about each kind of animal. Unfortunately, John didn't keep very good notes. When he got home he realized he had the following hodgepodge of information:

Animal #1: Is native to North America, doesn't have retractile claws, and doesn't spend a lot of time on land.

Animal #2: Is native to North America, walks on its toes, and spends almost all of its time on land.

Animal #3: Doesn't have retractile claws, walks on the flats of its feet, and spends almost all of its time on land.

Animal #4: Is native to North America, walks on its toes, and eats mostly meat.

Animal #5: Doesn't have retractile claws, walks on its toes, and eats meat and a lot of plants.

Animal #6: Doesn't have retractile claws, eats mostly meat, and spends almost all of its time on land.

Animal #7: Is native to North America, spends almost all of its time on land, doesn't have retractile claws, and walks on its toes.

After reading over his sketchy information, John is convinced that he can figure out which animal is which. He remembers that giant pandas eat mostly plants, gray foxes eat a lot of plants as well as meat, but all the other carnivores are pretty strict meat eaters; the bobcat is the only animal on his list that has retractile claws; giant pandas and hyenas are the only ones not native to North America; only polar bears and river otters spend most of their lives away from land; and only two of the animals are plantigrade—the polar bear and the giant panda.

Can you help John figure out which animal is which? And also "fill in the gaps" so each animal's information tells whether or not it:

- is native to North America
- has retractile claws
- spends almost all of its time on land
- is digitigrade
- is a strict meat eater

MAMMALS WITH HOOVES

O n the African savannah, a giraffe reaches up into the trees for a mouthful of leaves. In Yellowstone National Park, a herd of bison grazes on grass. And in a northeastern North American woodland, a moose wades along the shore of a small lake, munching on aquatic plants. These animals are just a few of the *ungulates* (UN-gyuh-luhts)—hooved mammals whose meals are made up almost entirely of plants.

BODY PLANS AND LIFESTYLES

Hoofin' It: All ungulates walk on hooved toes. Hooves are made of a hard bony substance called *keratin,* which encases an ungulate's toe bones. And depending on the number of toes that they walk on, most ungulates belong to one of two groups—the *even-toed* ungulates or the *odd-toed* ungulates. Horses and zebras (one toe), rhinoceroses (three toes), and tapirs (four toes on the front feet; three toes on the hind feet) are the only kinds of odd-toed ungulates. But there are many kinds of even-toed ungulates. Deer and camels (two toes) and hippopotamuses (four toes) are just a few examples of the mammals in the even-toed group.

Elephants are "primitive" ungulates, and their feet are a little bit different from those of the even- and odd-toed ungulates. These mammals have hooves on their toes, but most of their weight rests on flat, elastic pads rather than on the toes themselves.

horse

camel

hippopotamus

elephant

Fleet Feet: Many ungulates survive by outrunning their predators. For example, a horse can run at a speed of 30 miles (48 km) per hour for over four miles (6 km) without stopping. Hooves help ungulates run fast. And long muscular legs help give ungulates greater endurance and strength.

Eating Machines: Ungulates eat a variety of plants and plant parts including stems, leaves, fruits, flowers, seeds, bark, and twigs. Most of them have long muzzles that they use to reach their food. And many have strong lips and tongues that they use for grabbing and tearing off foliage and other vegetation. For example, a giraffe's tongue can reach out over 12 inches (30 cm) to wrap around and pull down leafy branches.

(continued next page)

giraffe

25

Super Senses: Most ungulates have well-developed senses. Their long noses are packed with olfactory nerves that help them detect predators. And many have ears that can rotate to detect sounds coming from all directions. Ungulates also have large eyes that are set on the sides of their heads. This lets them see in many directions at the same time.

The Same Old Grind: Besides talented tongues and super senses, ungulates have teeth that are well adapted to eating plants. Many ungulates have sharp incisors that they use to pluck or snip off plants. And all of them have molars that are broad and flat with raised ridges. When ungulates chew, they don't chew in an up-and-down circular motion the way people do. Instead, their strong jaw muscles move their molars in a side-to-side/front-to-back triangular motion. As the molars move across each other, they grind plant material just as a millstone grinds grain.

Special Stomachs: Some plant parts are difficult or even impossible for many mammals to digest. But ungulates have special stomachs and intestines that help them handle this tough food. *Ruminants,* such as giraffes, cattle, and almost all the other even-toed ungulates, have the most complex stomachs. When a ruminant swallows, its food goes to a stomach chamber where bacteria ferment it. This process helps break down the food chemically so that it can be absorbed later. After the food has fermented for awhile, the mammal regurgitates it and chews it again. This second chewing is called *rumination,* or "chewing the cud." The animal gradually swallows this twice-chewed food again, and the food ferments some more as it goes through three other stomach chambers and then the intestines. Because they chew, ferment, chew, and then ferment their food again, ruminants are able to break down the plant material almost entirely. But it may take four days to digest a meal completely.

Elephants and all of the odd-toed ungulates are *hindgut fermenters* and have much simpler stomachs than the ruminants. When they swallow their food, it passes from the stomach to an enlarged portion of the intestines. Here, bacteria ferment the food and the nutrients are absorbed. Food takes much less time to pass through the gut of hindgut fermenters. But these mammals don't break down the plants as completely as the ruminants do, so they must eat more to get the nutrients they need.

Safety in Numbers: Many species of ungulates feed on grasses in open areas where shelter from predators is scarce. And many of these mammals live in herds. As part of a herd, any one mammal is less likely to fall prey to an attacker. With so many alert eyes watching for danger, a predator may be spotted sooner and an alarm given so the whole herd can flee.

greater kudu

giraffe

pronghorn

beisa oryx

moose

A Trunkful of Fun

Make a life-sized paper elephant and imitate elephant movements and behaviors.

Objectives:
Compare the dimensions of elephant body parts to those of a human. Name three ways an elephant uses its trunk. Name two ways an elephant uses its ears.

Ages:
Primary and Intermediate

Materials:
- *index cards*
- *newspaper or butcher paper*
- *tape*
- *scissors*
- *tempera paint*
- *paintbrushes*
- *black marker*
- *pictures of elephants*
- *music*
- *rulers or yardsticks*

Subjects:
Science and Art

What would it be like to have a nose that's over seven feet (2 m) long? Or ears that stick out three and a half feet (1 m) from either side of your head? Only African elephants—largest of the land animals—know for sure. By working in groups to build a life-sized paper profile of an African elephant, your kids can get a feeling for the immense proportions of these mammals. And by doing the "Funky Trunk Dance," they can imitate the ways elephants use their huge and versatile trunks and ears.

PART 1: BUILD A PAPER PACHYDERM

Draw each of the miniature patterns shown below on a separate index card and include all dimensions. Then divide the kids into teams of two or three. Each team will be responsible for drawing and cutting out one of the elephant pattern pieces. Since the finished elephant will be a huge profile, you'll need only one tusk, one front and one back leg, and one ear. But you can make as many footprints as you want. Explain that the pattern pieces represent the dimensions that a large African bull (male) elephant might have.

Provide plenty of butcher paper or newspaper for the kids to work with. They'll also need lots of tape to make the larger pattern pieces. And of course, they'll need a large work area. (Depending on the number and ages of the kids you're working with, you might want to keep the level of activity to a minimum by having only one team work on their pattern piece at a time.) When they've finished taping and cutting, the kids can paint their elephant pieces.

(continued next page)

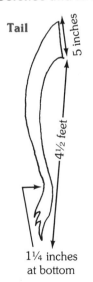

Tail

5 inches

4½ feet

1¼ inches at bottom

Note: Tail measurements given represent what the tail would look like from a side view. Viewed head-on, the tail would be about 10 inches wide at the base and about 2½ inches wide at the bottom.

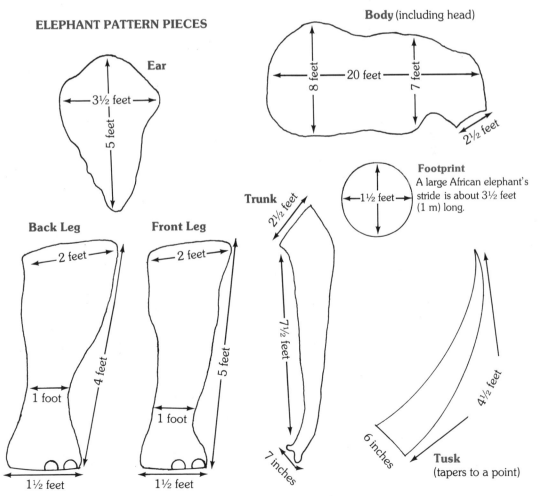

ELEPHANT PATTERN PIECES

Ear

3½ feet

5 feet

Body (including head)

8 feet — 20 feet — 7 feet

2½ feet

Back Leg

2 feet

4 feet

1 foot

1½ feet

Front Leg

2 feet

5 feet

1 foot

1½ feet

Trunk

2½ feet

7½ feet

7 inches

Footprint

1½ feet

A large African elephant's stride is about 3½ feet (1 m) long.

Tusk (tapers to a point)

6 inches

4½ feet

Luise Woelflein

Luise Woelflein

- Have the kids tape the footprints to the floor, the correct distance apart. Then have them compare their foot sizes and strides to that of an elephant.
- Hold up one of the elephant legs and have the kids stand next to it to see how their own legs "stack up" to it.
- Have each person carefully measure one of his or her upper incisors and figure out about how many times bigger an elephant's incisor (tusk) can be.
- Spread out an ear or the elephant body on the floor and have the kids see how many of them can sit or lie down in each one. (Be careful—the paper can tear easily.)

When you're ready for the kids to put the elephant together, tell them to lay the pattern pieces on the floor in the correct shape. Then have them tape the pieces together securely, using long strips of tape.

Once the elephant is all taped together, have the kids outline the ear and tusk with a black magic marker. Then enlist the help of another adult or two to carefully lift up the elephant and tape it to a wall.

Here are a few ideas for some comparisons the kids can make once they've made their elephant parts:
- Tape the elephant tail, trunk, or tusk to one wall and have the kids measure their height against it.

PART 2: DO THE FUNKY TRUNK DANCE

Start this activity by asking the kids if they can name some ways elephants use their trunks. As you show the kids pictures of elephants, explain that a trunk is basically just an oversized nose. But an elephant uses its long nose for more than just smelling. Here's a list of some elephant trunk talents:
- **Living Straws**—Elephants use their trunks to drink about 30 gallons (114 l) of water a day! They just suck the water up into their trunks and squirt it into their mouths. An adult elephant's trunk can hold about 1½ gallons (6 l) of water at a time.
- **Super Sprayers**—A trunk can serve as a built-in shower for elephants: Once the animals suck the water up, they can squirt it on themselves. "Showers" help elephants keep clean and—more importantly—stay cool.

    Elephants also suck up dust and spray it on themselves. Dust baths may help to get rid of insects and other pests.

- **Noisemakers**—When an elephant senses danger, it often *trumpets,* or makes shrill sounds through its outstretched trunk. Air columns in elephants' trunks help to amplify the trumpeting and other sounds the animals make.
- **Food Feelers**—Elephants' trunks are very sensitive organs of touch—just as human hands are. Elephants use their "feely" trunks to grasp objects such as fruits, leaves, tree bark, and other plant parts. Since these huge beasts can spend up to 20 hours a day feeding, their trunks stay busy finding food.
- **Hefty Haulers**—In India and some other parts of Asia, elephants are a real help to people. Trained elephants work in the logging industry, carrying loads on their backs and lifting and moving logs weighing as much as 600 pounds (270 kg) with their trunks.

Elephants also wave their trunks in the air as an aggressive threat, snore through them, and clean their ears with them.

Elephants' ears also have more than one use. For example, by flapping its ears an elephant can cool itself off. And by slapping its ears against its head it can call to its young or warn others of danger.

After discussing elephants and how they use their trunks and ears, put on some music and get the kids up on their feet to do the "Funky Trunk Dance." (Try getting hold of "Baby Elephant Walk" by Henry Mancini. It's part of the soundtrack of the 1962 movie entitled *Hatari!* and it's also featured on some other Henry Mancini records.) As you lead them around the room, call out different motions they can do with their "trunks" and "ears" (see photos on page 28). For example, you can have them pretend to take a "shower" or a dust bath. They can also trumpet a warning and take a drink. And they can create a cool breeze with their "ears" by flapping them back and forth.

A Horse of a Different Color

Make an accordion-style horse cut-out.

Objectives:
Define wild and tame. Name some mammals that have been tamed by people. Describe several types of horses.

Ages:
Primary and Intermediate

Materials:
- *crayons or colored pencils*
- *pictures of wild and tame horses*
- *copies of page 23*
- *scissors*

Subjects:
Social Studies and Art

Horses have always been one of the most popular and depended-on mammals in the world. In this short activity, your group can learn more about horses and how horses and other mammals were tamed from their wild ancestors.

First ask the children to think of all the ways people use horses today or have used them in the past, and make a list of what they come up with. (transportation, recreation, companionship, food, and so on)

Explain that the horses we know today evolved from prehistoric mammals that looked more like racing dogs than horses. Show the kids pictures of some of the early horses. Explain that it wasn't until about four million years ago (which is pretty recent, in terms of geologic history) that horses started looking as they do today. By that time they had developed larger bodies, stronger legs, teeth that were adapted for chewing grass, and sturdier hooves.

Mammalogists know that primitive people hunted horses and ate their meat. But they are not sure exactly when people first began to tame horses. Some scientists think the first horses were tamed and bred in captivity about 5000 years ago.

Ask the kids if they can explain the difference between a wild animal and a tame (domestic) one. Explain that tame animals are cared for by people. These animals get the food, water, and shelter they need from people and don't have to rely on their own instincts to stay alive. Wild animals, on the other hand, are not cared for by people and survive on their own in the wild.

Ask the kids to name other tame animals. (pigs, cows, dogs, cats, goats, sheep, and so on) Ask why people tame animals. (Animals provide people with food, companionship, recreation, transportation, clothing, and so on. By taming animals, people can breed them for special qualities, such as thick fur, tender meat, docile personalities, and tasty milk.)

Show the children pictures of some of the breeds of horses that people have developed over the years. Explain that by mating horses that have special qualities, new breeds of horses can be developed. For example, Arabian, Shetland Pony, Appaloosa, Morgan, and Clydesdale are

Przewalski's horse

Leonard Lee Rue IV

different breeds of domestic horses. Then show the kids pictures of wild members of the horse family, such as the zebra, African wild ass, and Przewalski's horse. Explain that all breeds of the domestic horses we have today came from wild ancestors, as did some of their wild relatives, such as the zebra, African wild ass, and Przewalski's horse.

Now pass out copies of page 23. Have the children cut out the horses, following the directions on page 18. Tell them they can color them to show some of the different breeds of modern horses or some of the wild members of the horse family.

BRANCHING OUT: MORE MAMMAL CUT-OUTS

Have the kids make their own mammal cut-outs. They can make a chain of goats, sheep, pigs, cows, dogs, or other type of domestic animal, or they can create a wild mammal cut-out.

Horns and Antlers

Use paper-mache, wire, and paint to make antler and horn models.

Objectives:
Describe the difference between horns and antlers. Define grazer and browser. Explain some of the ways mammals use their horns and antlers.

Ages:
Intermediate and Advanced

Materials:
- *copies of page 32*
- *flour (5-10 pounds)*
- *warm water*
- *lots of newspaper*
- *washtub or large bucket*
- *several small buckets*
- *large mixing spoon*
- *sturdy shoeboxes or other small boxes*
- *medium gauge steel wire or coat hangers*
- *scissors*
- *wire cutters*
- *small paper drinking cups*
- *tape*
- *tempera paint*
- *paintbrushes*
- *pictures of mammals with horns and antlers*
- *white paper towels*

Hooves aren't the only thing that sets the hooved mammals apart from other mammals. Many of the "hoofers" also have antlers or horns. In this activity, your group will find out more about horns and antlers by making models of the antlers and horns of some even-toed ungulates. (Odd-toed ungulates, such as horses, tapirs, and rhinos, do not have true horns or antlers. For more about odd- and even-toed ungulates, see page 25.)

reticulated giraffe
Leonard Lee Rue III

Several days before the activity, ask the children to find and bring in *sturdy*, small boxes about the size of a shoebox or slightly larger. (You will need one box for every three children.) When you're ready to start the activity, pass out copies of page 32 and ask the children what the mammals shown have in common. Point out that each has either horns or antlers. Explain that a horn is a slow-growing, permanent bone, covered by a thin layer of hard material. Horns are usually not branched. Ask the children to find the animals pictured that have horns. (bighorn sheep, bison, markhor, impala, musk ox, and cape buffalo) Explain that antlers are also made of bone, but they are fast-growing. Antlers are also not permanent. Animals that have antlers shed them and grow a new set each year. And unlike horns, antlers are often elaborately branched. Ask the kids to find the mammals on the page that have antlers. (elk, caribou, whitetail deer, moose)

You might want to mention that there are a few exceptions to these generalizations. For example, a giraffe's horns are covered with skin and hair, not hard material. And a rhinoceros' horn isn't bone at all—it's a densely-packed mass of hardened hair fibers, and is not considered a true horn.

Ask the kids whether it is the male or the female mammals that have horns and antlers. Explain that antlers are usually

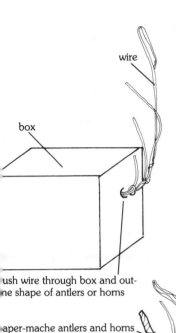

wire

box

ush wire through box and out-
ne shape of antlers or horns

aper-mache antlers and horns

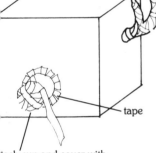

tape

tach cup and cover with
aper-mache

found only on males and are often used for defense and in battles between rival males during the mating season. (The caribou is an exception. Both males and females have antlers.) Horns may be found on both sexes and are used for defense as well as by males in mating fights.

Then ask the kids what they think the animals on the page eat. Explain that all the animals pictured are plant eaters. Some feed almost exclusively on grass, while others eat bark, twigs, buds, and other shrub and tree parts. Tell the kids that hooved mammals that feed mainly on grass and other small plants are called *grazers*. And those that feed on twigs, bark, buds, and other tree and shrub parts are called *browsers*. Also point out that many hooved mammals graze at certain times of the year and browse at other times.

Now divide the group into teams of three and have each team pick a number from 1 to 10 out of a sack. Tell the kids that they will be making a paper-mache model of the hooved mammal whose number on the Copycat Page matches the number they picked. Also point out the questions on the Copycat Page. Explain that after each team has built the model of their mammal's head, they must make a presentation to the rest of the group in which they answer the question that corresponds to their mammal. In their presentations they should also tell how the animal uses its horns or antlers, what the animal eats, and any other interesting folklore, history, or science facts they want to include.

Have the kids in each team research their mammals, finding pictures that show the horns or antlers from several different angles. Give each team wire and a sturdy box, and provide several wire cutters for the group. Be sure to spread plastic, cloth, or newspaper on the floor of the work area. Here's how to make the models:

1. Push a length of wire through the box so that it sticks out on both sides. Add more wire, bending as needed, to outline the shape and branches of the horns or antlers (see diagram). If the horns or antlers start to tip over, tape them in place.
2. Once the wiring is done, mix the paper-mache paste in a large washtub or bucket. Gradually add 10-20 cups (2-5 l) of warm water to five pounds (2.3 kg) of flour, forming a thick paste.
3. Scoop the paste into smaller buckets, and cut newspaper into strips 6-8 inches (15-20 cm) long.
4. Dip the strips of paper into the paste and apply them to the wires to form the horns and antlers.
5. Tape paper cups to the front of the heads and cover with paper-mache to form snouts (see diagram).
6. To smooth out the paper-mache, add a final layer of white paper towels.
7. Let the heads dry for several days and then paint.

While their models are drying, have the kids prepare their presentations. They can write short reports, draw pictures, or make maps or charts. After the presentations, go over all the questions and answers.

ANSWERS TO COPYCAT PAGE

1. By counting the deep grooves on a ram's horns, you can tell the animal's age: Each groove represents one year.
2. Cape buffalo don't have many sweat glands. They keep cool by swimming or taking a mud bath.
3. Velvet is a layer of skin and hair that covers the antlers of deer and other mammals as the antlers are growing. During the rutting season, a deer's velvet dries up and the animal scrapes or rubs it off.
4. No. Caribou feed on whatever types of food are available in each season. For example, after spring thaw they feed on new plant growth. In summer, they feed on the leaves of shrubs and trees. After the first hard frost, they will switch to lichens and the leaves of evergreen shrubs. And in winter, they eat twigs of certain trees and shrubs and dig in the snow to find winter greens.
5. Wapiti is another name for elk.
6. A moose's bell is a large fold of skin that hangs from the moose's throat.
7. Rival males use their horns in fights to see which male is stronger.
8. Markhors are a type of goat.
9. Musk oxen form a line or a circle to defend themselves. When a predator gets too close the adults will often take turns driving it away.
10. Impalas often escape from predators by making high, long jumps. Some can jump 10 feet (3 m) high and broad jump 30 feet (9 m).

1. Bighorn Sheep
How can you tell the age of a bighorn sheep ram?

2. Cape Buffalo
How do cape buffalo keep cool?

3. Whitetail Deer
What does velvet have to do with whitetail deer?

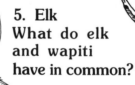

5. Elk
What do elk and wapiti have in common?

4. Caribou
Do caribou feed on the same food all year?

6. Moose
What is a moose's bell?

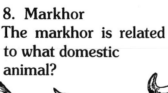

8. Markhor
The markhor is related to what domestic animal?

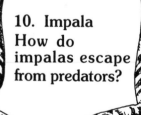

10. Impala
How do impalas escape from predators?

7. Bison
How do male bison use their horns?

9. Musk Ox
What does a herd of musk oxen do when confronted by attackers?

RANGER RICK'S NATURESCOPE: AMAZING MAMMALS

BATS

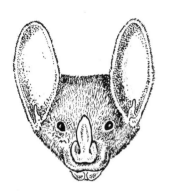

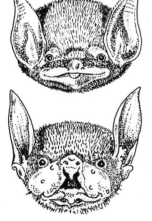

Some catch fish. Some eat scorpions. Some lap blood. Some swim. Some crawl. Some jump and hop. Some migrate hundreds of miles. Some live to be more than 30 years old. And all of them fly. Yes, bats can do all of these things and more. Although many people lump all bats together, there are actually nearly 1000 different species of bats, making them one of the most diverse mammal groups in the world. In this chapter we'll look at some of the amazing members of the bat group and compare their strategies for staying alive.

Wings and Things: Unlike all other mammals, bats have true wings and can fly. Their wings are actually modified arms, which are somewhat similar to human arms. Just like humans, bats have large upper arm bones that connect to their shoulders. But their forearms are unusually long, and four of their fingers stretch out to form the foundation of the wing (see diagram on next page). A skinlike membrane, thinner than the thickness of a plastic bag, covers the fingers and forearms and stretches to the shorter hindlegs and feet. Although this thin wing membrane sometimes covers the tail, it never covers the claws on the hind feet or the thumb.

Even though bats are super fliers, they can get around in other ways too. The powerful claws that many bats have on their thumbs allow them to climb along rocky cave walls, tree branches, and other surfaces. Bats can also walk on the ground, supporting themselves on the joints of their wrists, with their wings folded tightly to their sides. And most bats can swim, using their wings as paddles.

Bats also do something that most other animals can't—they hang upside down for long periods of time. Using the sharp, curved claws on their hindlegs as hooks, they can hang from branches, overhangs, and ledges. Some bats also have suckerlike discs on their thumbs and feet that allow them to stick to smooth surfaces.

Dividing the Bats: You won't find any bats in Antarctica. But you will find them on every other continent. Mammalogists have divided the bats of the world into two main groups: the *megabats* and the *microbats*. Although the two groups are separated from each other because they have different wing, claw, and skull characteristics, many of the bats in both groups look alike and have similar habits. Generally, the megabats are larger than the microbats, have better eyesight, eat fruit, nectar, or pollen, and usually do not hibernate. Microbats, on the other hand, are usually smaller, rely on their ears more than their eyes to find food, eat mainly insects, and usually hibernate in winter. But some microbats are fruit eaters.

Most of the large megabats, such as flying foxes and other fruit-eating bats, live in tropical parts of Australia, Asia, Africa, and the Pacific. The smaller insect eaters are found in the Americas, as well as throughout Europe, Asia, Africa, and Australia.

Bugs, Blossoms, and Blood: Bats feed on a variety of foods, including frogs, fish, birds, insects, fruit, nectar, pollen, and blood. And each type of bat is adapted to its own feeding specialty. For example, some fruit bats have long tongues for probing deep into blossoms to lap up nectar. Vampire bats have special heat sensory organs on their faces that allow them to locate blood vessels on their prey. And fishing bats grab slippery fish with special hooklike claws.

(continued next page)

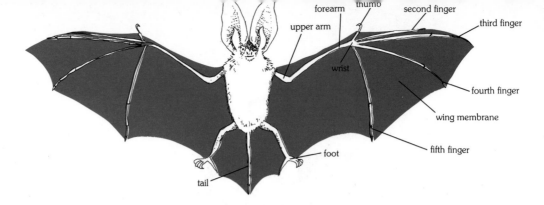

upper arm • forearm • thumb • second finger • third finger • wrist • fourth finger • wing membrane • fifth finger • foot • tail

Bouncing Off the Walls: Many of the small microbats have an amazing way of catching insects and other prey. Instead of using their *eyes* to spot food, they use their ears to listen for it. These bats make a series of high-pitched, squeaking sounds (usually too high-pitched for human ears to hear) that bounce off objects nearby. By listening to the returning echoes, these bats can judge the distance to objects in their path. Using this *echolocation* system, bats can catch fast-flying insects or darting fish, and at the same time avoid branches, wires, and other obstacles. (Several other types of mammals, including dolphins, shrews, and tenrecs, use echolocation to find food too.) Bats also make noises that people *can* hear, from whining and clicking sounds to loud twitters and squeaks.

Waiting Out the Winter: How do microbats make it through the winter? Some "sleep" through it, hibernating in caves, buildings, or other shelters. Others move to warmer, insect-rich areas.

The hibernators usually choose a spot that maintains a fairly constant temperature throughout the winter. (That's why caves are so popular.) Looking like furry carpets, many bats hibernate in huge groups, although some species hibernate alone. And sometimes two or three different species hibernate together, hanging side by side. As hibernation begins, a bat's internal system slows way down. Their body temperature may fall from 104° F (40° C) to lower than 32° F (0° C) and their breathing can go from 200 breaths a minute to fewer than 25. And during hibernation, as their fat reserves vanish, their plump little bodies shrink like slowly deflating balloons.

Migrating bats often travel hundreds of miles to escape cold weather and find the food they need. Some travel in huge flocks, migrating with birds that also are heading south for the winter. Others travel in smaller groups and go much shorter distances. (Fruit-eating bats of the tropics migrate only when fruit, nectar, or pollen supplies are depleted.)

Bat Babies: Home life for a young bat varies, depending on the type of bat. Some bats grow up in crowded maternity caves, with tens of thousands of other bat babies and mothers. Others grow up in small groups or alone with their mother in a sheltered spot.

Most bats are born tiny, wrinkled, and naked. And unlike many types of baby mammals, bat pups often have a full set of milk teeth at birth. These tiny teeth have hooked ends that enable baby bats to cling to their mothers' teats. Although some fruit bat babies will hitch a ride on Mom when she flies off to look for a meal, other bat pups are left "hanging around" at home until they are old enough to fly.

Not Batting a Thousand: Although bats are getting better press than they once did, most people still don't realize how important bats are to the world's ecology and how harmless they are to people. Not only are bats great insect eaters, they are also important pollinators—especially of plants in the tropics. But like many mammals, bats in many areas are having a difficult time surviving because of habitat loss and other problems. Some are killed for food. Others succumb to pesticide poisoning or disturbances from spelunkers and well-meaning biologists. And many are killed out of fear or ignorance.

Bat and Moth

Play an echolocation game and solve a bat math problem.

Objective:
Describe how insect-eating bats catch prey in the dark.

Ages:
Primary and Intermediate

Materials:
- *blindfolds*
- *copies of page 44 (Part 3)*
- *pencils and paper*

Subject:
Science

In this game, your kids can simulate how bats use echolocation to catch moths and other insects. (For more about echolocation, see "Ears in the Dark" on page 39.) To play, have the kids form a circle about 10-15 feet (3-4.5 m) across. Choose one member of the group to play the role of a bat. Blindfold the bat, and have him or her stand in the center of the circle. Then designate three to five other children as moths and have them also come to the center. The object of the game is for the bat to try to tag as many moths as possible. Both the bat and moths can move, but they must stay within the circle. (Once a moth is tagged, he or she should go outside the circle and sit down.)

Whenever the bat calls out "bat," the moths have to respond by calling back "moth." Tell the moths that every time they hear the bat call "bat," it simulates the bat sending out an ultrasonic pulse to see what's in its path. The pulse bounces off the moths and echoes back to the bat, simulated by the moths calling out "moth."

The bat must listen carefully, concentrate to find out where the moths are, and try to tag them. To add more excitement, you can designate two children to be bats at the same time. Just watch to make sure the two bats don't collide with each other. You might want to pick a short and tall child so they don't bump heads.

As another variation, you can add obstacles by designating several children to play trees. When the bat calls out "bat," the moths must call out "moth" and the trees must call out "tree." If a bat runs into a tree as it tries to tag a moth, the bat is out.

(Idea reprinted and adapted with permission from *Sharing Nature With Children* by Joseph Cornell, Ananda Publications, 1979.)

(continued next page)

Dan Kowal

BRANCHING OUT: BAT MATH

As a challenge, see if your group can figure out the bat math problem at the bottom of page 44. Here's how it's done:

1. To find out how much of a little brown bat's nightly food consists of mosquitoes (in grams):
   4 grams of food per night
   × .20 (mosquitoes are 20% of a bat's diet) = .80 grams of mosquitoes per night

2. To find out the number of mosquitoes eaten by a little brown bat in one night:
   - Convert .80 grams of mosquitoes to milligrams—
   .80 × 1000 (there are 1000 milligrams per gram) = 800 milligrams of mosquitoes per night
   - Divide the number of milligrams of mosquitoes by the weight of one mosquito—

800 milligrams of mosquitoes per night divided by 2.2 milligrams per mosquito = 364 mosquitoes eaten in one night

3. To find out how many mosquitoes are eaten during the three-month summer season:
   - Multiply 90 nights by the number of mosquitoes eaten in one night—
   90 × 364 = 32,760 or about 33,000 mosquitoes eaten by one little brown bat during the summer

Note: Explain to the kids that this number is just an approximate figure. Also explain that most scientific research is recorded in metrics, not English measure.

(Math problem reprinted with permission from *Rhode Island . . . Naturally: Mammals* by Roger and Gail Greene, Audubon Society of Rhode Island, 1982.)

A Bat Like That

Compare two bat poems and discuss how people's attitudes toward bats differ. Discuss some amazing bat trivia.

Objectives:
List some of the reasons many people don't like bats. Explain why bats are important to people and other animals.

Ages:
Intermediate and Advanced

Materials:
- *copies of pages 42 and 43*
- *chalkboard or easel paper*
- *markers*

Subjects:
Science and Language Arts

vampire bat

Marilyn K. Krog

Say the word "bat" and most people cringe. But the fear and disgust that many people feel toward bats is unfounded. Bats are actually gentle and intelligent and, contrary to popular belief, rarely transmit rabies. In this two-part activity, your group will get a chance to explore their feelings about bats and find out more about these amazing flying mammals.

PART 1: WHAT'S A BAT?

Start by listing the words and phrases shown on the next page on a chalkboard or large piece of easel paper. (Don't write down the answers, which are shown in parentheses.) Then have the kids decide as a group whether each word or phrase describes all bats, some bats, or no bats and write the word *all, some,* or *none* next to each phrase.

black or brown (some)
warm-blooded (all)
larger than a mouse (some)
eat insects (some)
hang upside down (all)
make sounds people can't hear (some)
eat fish (some)
orange (some)
walk on the ground (some)
suck blood (none, but some lap blood)
swim (some)
hibernate (some)
cold-blooded (none)
migrate (some)
nest in people's hair (none)
active at night (some)
spread rabies (some)
make sounds people can hear (all)
live more than 30 years (some)
eat fruit (some)

Leave the list up and tell the kids that they will find out later how many they got right. Then pass out copies of page 42. Explain that bats are a very diverse group of mammals and that there are nearly 1000 different species in the world. Have the kids try to fill in the letter of the correct answer on their sheets as you read each question and the multiple choice answers listed below. (An asterisk indicates the correct answer.) Discuss each question as you go along, as well as the other trivia facts listed on the page.

Afterward, go back to the original list of words and phrases and check to see how many the group got right.

(continued next page)

BAT TRIVIA

1. The largest bats in the world are the flying foxes of Australia and Southeast Asia. Many of these fruit- and nectar-eating bats have furry, foxlike faces and wingspans that stretch _____.
   a. about a foot
   b. about three feet
   c. about six feet*

2. The smallest mammal in the world is a bat called the bumble bee bat. It weighs _____ and its body is slightly larger than a jelly bean.
   a. more than an orange
   b. about the same as a half dollar
   c. less than a dime*

3. Some bats live in colonies made up of more than _____ individuals.
   a. 20 million*
   b. 2 billion
   c. 100,000

4. Many bats have unusual facial features, such as huge ears and strange nose flaps, that _____.
   a. help them fly
   b. help them attract a mate
   c. help them navigate and find food*

5. Most bats feed on insects. Some can catch over _____ fruit flies in an hour.
   a. 1000*
   b. 250
   c. 10,000

6. Female bats usually give birth hanging upside down. Their normal litter size is _____.
   a. 5-7
   b. 1*
   c. more than 10

7. Vampire bats use their sharp incisors to make a tiny slit in their prey's skin. As blood oozes out, they lap it up. These bats usually feed on the blood of _____.
   a. people
   b. reptiles and very small mammals
   c. large birds and mammals*

8. Nectar-feeding bats have long tongues with feathery tips that reach deep into night-blooming flowers. Many of these long-tongued bats are important plant pollinators in _____.
   a. parts of North America only
   b. parts of Asia and Australia only
   c. all tropical parts of the world*

PART 2: BAT POETRY

Pass out copies of page 43 and have the kids read both poems and compare them, using these discussion questions as guidelines:

- What feelings did you get from each poem?
- How are the poems different? How are they alike?
- Which poem agrees most with how you feel about bats?
- Do you think both poems are scientifically accurate? Why or why not?

As you discuss the poems, you might want to ask the kids how poetry expresses feelings and facts differently from prose. (Poetry combines the sound [meter and rhyme] and meaning of language to create ideas and express feelings and facts. Unlike most poetry, prose usually has no regular meter or rhyme.)

As a follow-up, have the kids try to write their own bat poems, focusing on bats in general or on a specific type of bat. Have the kids illustrate their poems and read them to the rest of the group.

BRANCHING OUT: MAKE A BAT MOBILE

After writing bat poems, have your kids make their own bat mobiles using sweet gum balls or pinecones, acorn caps, and black construction paper. For directions, see "Bat Mobile," *Ranger Rick,* October 1981.

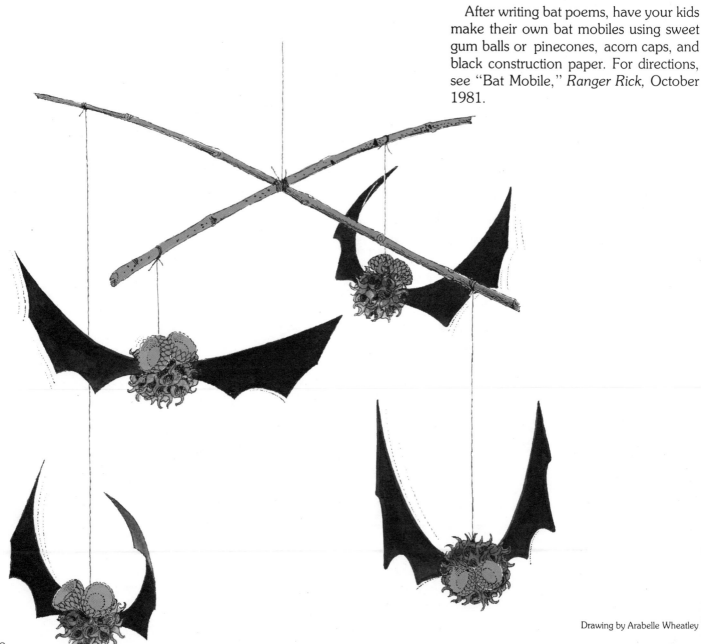

Drawing by Arabelle Wheatley

Ears in the Dark

Discuss how scientists learned about echolocation and design a "sound-catcher."

Objectives:
Compare hypotheses about how bats echolocate and describe how insect-eating bats catch prey in the dark. Design and test a sound-enhancer.

Ages:
Intermediate and Advanced

Materials:
- *copies of page 44*
- *chalkboard or easel paper (optional)*
- *cardboard, glue, construction paper, and other art supplies*
- *pictures of insect-eating bats*

Subject:
Science

atching moths and mosquitoes in the dark is no easy task—unless you happen to be an insect-eating bat. About 700 different species of bats catch insects using a system called *echolocation*. (For more about echolocation, see page 34.) This two-part activity will introduce your group to echolocation and the incredible lives of insect-eating bats.

PART 1: THE BIG BAT MYSTERY

Pass out a copy of page 44 to each person and have the kids read Part 1. Afterward, discuss what a hypothesis is and how scientists design experiments to test their hypotheses. In this example, you can give the kids some help by asking them to think about how bats and owls are different, based on what Spallanzani observed. Tell them to think about the ways he could have tested his ideas about how bats navigate in the dark.

Discuss the hypotheses that the kids came up with and the ways they would test them. Then, using the following information, talk about how Spallanzani and the scientists that lived after him actually figured out how bats' and owls' methods of catching prey differ and how bats navigate in the dark. (You might want to outline major points on a chalkboard or large piece of easel paper to help the kids follow along.)

SOLVING THE MYSTERY OF ECHOLOCATION

At first Spallanzani thought both owls and bats relied on keen night vision to get around in the dark. To test this he placed a lightproof hood over the heads of the bats. When these bats tried to fly, they bumped into obstacles. Ask the kids what this showed. (From this experiment, it seemed that bats must use their eyes to navigate, because when their eyes were covered they bumped into obstacles.)

Next ask the kids if there was something incomplete about this experiment. Explain that even though this seemed to prove bats relied on vision to get around, Spallanzani did not use a *control*. Ask if someone can explain what is meant by a control, and if not, give them an example.

Explain that a control is usually carried out as part of an experiment and is identical in all respects to the experiment except that the variable being evaluated is unchanged. For example, if you are testing a hypothesis that states that green plants need sunlight, you could design an experiment to test this by putting one plant in a dark room and another on a sunny window ledge. In order for the experiment to be valid, both plants would need to have all other variables identical, such as the same amount of water, the same type and amount of nutrients in the soil, the same temperature, the same humidity, etc. In this case, the plant in the sunlight acts as the control. *(continued next page)*

Explain that Spallanzani knew he needed to set up a control using helmets that were not lightproof. When he placed these transparent hoods on the bats, they still couldn't fly without crashing into obstacles. Ask the kids what this proved. Explain that this proved that even when they could see, bats still bumped into things when flying in the dark. So bats must use something besides vision to help them navigate.

To prove that bats do not rely on vision, as owls do, Spallanzani surgically removed the eyes from some of the bats. Ask the kids to guess what happened when he released the blind bats in the dark. To his surprise, they flew as well as the sighted bats, and when he analyzed the contents of their stomachs, he found that all the bats had about the same number of insects in them. Based on his experiments, Spallanzani hypothesized that bats use some kind of special hearing system to help them navigate.

Other scientists conducted more experiments to find out how bats navigate. A Swiss scientist plugged the ears of some bats with wax and found they crashed into obstacles. The bats with unplugged ears were able to get around with no trouble.

Explain that the results of all of this research were written down but ignored for about 100 years due to another hypothesis that was proposed by a French scientist, Dr. Cuvier. Dr. Cuvier hypothesized that bats had a super sense of touch and that sensitive nerves and delicate hairs on their wings and bodies gave bats a special "sixth" sense. This special sense of touch, he reasoned, helped bats navigate in the dark. Ask the kids to suggest experiments that might be used to determine if bats use touch or hearing to get around.

Unfortunately people listened to Cuvier's theory, even though it was never scientifically proven. Explain that scientific discoveries sometimes get sidetracked, as Spallanzani's did, because research is not reviewed or believed.

The next bat theory came in the early 1900s. After the *Titanic* collided with a huge iceberg and sank, killing hundreds of people, an inventor named Sir Hiram Maxim developed a sonar warning device to help ships detect hidden underwater dangers. The sonar device sent out a series of low-frequency pulses (too low for people to hear). When the sounds hit an underwater obstacle, the returning echo was detected by the sonar tracking device and a bell would ring to warn the ship of possible danger. Sir Hiram hypothesized that bats used a similar "sonar" system. He thought that bats made very low noises

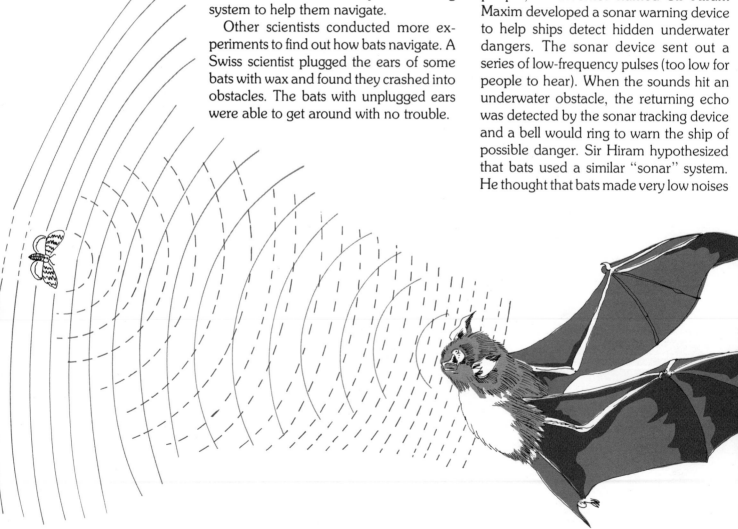

as they beat their wings, and that as these low sounds bounced off obstacles and prey, the bats could analyze the returning echoes to figure out what was where.

Sir Hiram was getting close to figuring out how bats navigate. They do use an echo detection system, as he thought. But they don't emit low-frequency pulses from their wingbeats.

The answer to the mystery finally came in the 1930s when a device was invented that could detect high-frequency sounds called ultrasounds. Donald Griffin, a biology student at Harvard who was interested in bats, thought he could prove how bats navigate by using this newly invented machine. He hypothesized that bats actually make a series of high-pitched sounds from their noses and/or mouths and that bats can interpret the returning echoes these sounds make as they bounce off obstacles. To test his theory, he put a cageful of bats near the new ultrasound detector and saw that he was correct: The bats were sending out continuous high-pitched beeps that were far too high for the human ear to hear. He hypothesized that these high-pitched beeps collided with trees, wires, insects, and other objects and sent back echoes that the bat could interpret. By piecing together the echo patterns, bats can form a "sound picture" of their environment.

So it was more than 130 years after Spallanzani's first experiments that the mystery was finally solved. And since then, scientists have learned much more about the complicated echolocation system that helps bats get around in the dark (see page 34).

PART 2: CAN YOU HEAR ME?

As scientists studied insect-eating bats around the world, they saw that different kinds of bats have different physical features that help them find food and avoid obstacles. For example, some bats, such as leaf-nosed bats, have very strange flaps of skin on their noses. These flaps act as resonators that help the bats project ultrasonic beeps through their noses. Many bats also have huge ears that help them detect returning echoes.

Have the kids read Part 2 on the Copycat Page. Then have them work alone or in small groups, using a variety of art supplies, to design their own soundcatchers. Explain that they will have to show that their devices improve their hearing.

When the kids are finished, have each person (or team) present his or her invention to the rest of the group. Also have them demonstrate how it works. Emphasize that this is a very rough way of testing the devices and that scientists would conduct much more accurate tests to actually demonstrate that something works.

As a follow-up, show the children pictures of mouse-eared bats, long-eared bats, and other bats that have oversized ears. Explain that large external ears help collect sound waves and funnel them to the middle and inner ears. Many of the returning echoes are very faint—sometimes over 200 times fainter than the original pulse. And large ears help bats amplify the weak returning echoes, giving bats a more detailed "picture" of the environment.

BRANCHING OUT: TAKE A BAT WALK

If you live in an area where there are insect-eating bats, take a twilight or night walk to see them in action. Find a bright street or porch light where insects are swarming, and watch to see if a bat is out hunting. (After your bat walk, you might want to have your group try the bat math problem at the bottom of page 44. See page 36 for the answer to the problem.) *Note:* Bat Conservation International sells bat detectors that make bat echolocation audible. For information, write to Bat Conservation International, P.O. Box 162603, Austin, TX 78716.

1. The largest bats in the world are the flying foxes of Australia and Southeast Asia. Many of these fruit- and nectar-eating bats have furry, foxlike faces and wingspans that stretch _____.

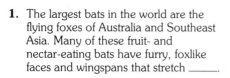

5. Most bats feed on insects. Some can catch over _____ fruit flies in an hour.

Not all bats are black or brown. Some have red, tan, olive-green, blue-gray, white, yellow, and even orange fur.

Some fishing bats use echolocation to find minnows. These bats have special hooklike claws that grip their squirming, slippery prey.

6. Female bats usually give birth hanging upside down. Their normal litter size is _____.

There are bats that eat frogs, mice, scorpions, birds, and even other bats.

2. The smallest mammal in the world is a bat called the bumble bee bat. It weighs _____ and its body is slightly larger than a jelly bean.

7. Vampire bats use their sharp incisors to make a tiny slit in their prey's skin. As blood oozes out, they lap it up. These bats usually feed on the blood of _____.

3. Some bats live in colonies made up of more than _____ individuals.

Mexican free-tailed bats are among the fastest-flying bats in the world. They are also great travelers. Some migrate over 825 miles (1300 km) from their summer homes to their winter roosting sites.

Many bats hibernate in caves and other protected places during the winter. During hibernation, some bats lose as much as 30% of their body weight.

Almost all bats are active at night. During the day, most sleep in communal roosting sites.

4. Many bats have unusual facial features, such as huge ears and strange nose flaps, that _____.

8. Nectar-feeding bats have long tongues with feathery tips that reach deep into night-blooming flowers. Many of these long-tongued bats are important plant pollinators in _____.

BEHOLD THE BAT

Bats are ugly, ugly, ugly,
Grotesque little faces,
Warty snouts,
Tiny teeth in alien mouths.
Friends of witches, friends of trolls,
Wrinkled parchment wings unfold,
Stretched-out finger bones and skin,
So very, very, batlike thin.
Darkness makes bats come alive,
Hairy bodies, piercing eyes.
Darting, swooping, diving demons,
Of caves and graves and hidden dens,
Moonlight madness, high-pitched beeps,
Bats give human beings the creeps.

BAT WATCHING

Some people are horse fans,
Others love cats,
And some like snakes and their kin.
But I love bats,
With their furry snouts,
And stretched-out wings of skin.

Can you imagine
How hard it would be
To catch hundreds of darting flies,
Or nab tiny moths
On the wing in the dark
Without ever using your eyes?

Or think about hanging
All day by your feet,
With your body turned upside down.
The world must look different
From a bat's point of view,
With everything twisted around.

But hanging around
Is only for days,
'Cause when twilight fades into night,
Many bats hit the skies
In search of flies
And other insect delights.

So while most other people
Are fast asleep,
With their cats and dogs cuddled tight,
I'm out walking,
Late at night,
Watching bats swoop around at a light.

PART 1: SPOTLIGHT ON SPALLANZANI

In 1793, long before computers and many other kinds of sophisticated equipment were invented, an Italian scientist named Lazzaro Spallanzani (SPAH-luhn-ZAH-nee) began an experiment. He wanted to find out how nocturnal creatures were able to get around in the dark. By bringing owls into his lab and releasing them in the dark, he learned that they were expert nighttime flyers—as long as there was some light present. But they couldn't fly in complete darkness.

On the other hand, he found that insect-eating bats had no trouble zipping about in complete darkness. Unlike the owls he had studied, the bats could avoid obstacles and snatch up prey (insects) without any light present at all.

If you were Lazzaro Spallanzani, what conclusions would you make from these observations? Come up with a hypothesis that would explain your conclusions. How could you test your hypothesis to see if your ideas were correct?

PART 2: DESIGN YOUR OWN SOUND-CATCHER

Your company has just given you an assignment: Design something that can help humans hear better. You are allowed to use construction paper, cardboard, or any other supplies you can think of. First make your invention, then demonstrate that it works.

PART 3: BAT MATH

Problem: How many mosquitoes does a little brown bat eat during one summer?

Given:
- A bat eats approximately 4 grams of insects in one night.

- At least 20% of a little brown bat's food consists of mosquitoes.

- A mosquito weighs approximately 2.2 milligrams.

- The summer season lasts for approximately 90 days.

RODENTS AND OTHER GNAWERS

Some of them sprint at speeds of up to 50 miles (80 km) per hour, others live a lifetime without ever drinking water, and some build dams and homes that can change the paths of streams and rivers. They are the *rodents* (mice, rats, squirrels, and others) and *lagomorphs* (rabbits, hares, and pikas), and they live in every type of habitat and on every continent except Antarctica. In this chapter we'll look at what makes these "choppers and hoppers" so special.

Endless Teeth: Imagine having teeth that never stop growing and that, without a good daily grinding, would lengthen until they grew right into your skull! Many rodents and lagomorphs have such teeth—"rootless" incisors and cheek teeth that grow continuously, just as our fingernails and hair do. But they keep their teeth at a reasonable length by gnawing on wood and other hard materials.

Because rodents' and lagomorphs' teeth look similar superficially, mammalogists lumped the animals together for many years. But as mammalogists continued to study these two groups of animals, they discovered some differences in the arrangement of their teeth and in the ways their skeletons are put together. They came to the conclusion that the two groups aren't closely related at all, and they split the animals into two separate orders. Here's a look at each:

RODENTS
Rodents and More Rodents: There's a lot of variety among the relatives of the house mouse that may live in your kitchen pantry. That's not too surprising, considering the fact there are more than 1500 species of rodents. No other group of mammals has this many representatives.

Rodents range in size from the .2-ounce (6-gm) harvest mouse to the 146-pound (66-kg) capybara, and they live in all kinds of habitats—from humid rain forests to sweltering deserts to snowy tundras. And depending on where they live, rodents can get around by burrowing, gliding, swimming, leaping, hopping, or running.

(continued next page)

red squirrel

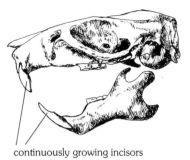

continuously growing incisors

Champion Chewers: A major part of the rodent "success story" can be attributed to these mammals' chisel-shaped incisors. Depending on the species, rodents may use their incisors to pierce hard-shelled nuts, gnaw through tough tree bark, snip off stems and grasses, or dig through hard-packed soil. And because they never stop growing, these super-sharp teeth last throughout a rodent's lifetime.

Jaws That Gnaw: Rodents also have strong muscles that pull their lower jaw forward and back in a unique gnawing motion. Scientists have divided the rodents into three main groups, based on the ways these jaw muscles are arranged:

- Squirrel-like rodents: squirrels, pocket gophers, beavers, and others
- Mouselike rodents: mice, rats, gerbils, and others
- Porcupinelike rodents: porcupines, guinea pigs, and others

There's Strength in Numbers: If food is plentiful, many rodents have the potential to reproduce at a phenomenal rate. For example, once a female Norway lemming reaches sexual maturity, she could theoretically produce a litter of seven every three or four weeks for the rest of her life. Because they can be so abundant, rodents are often an important part of many predators' diets.

Not all rodents are so prolific, though. Beavers, for example, raise only one or two kits a year. And capybaras and guinea pigs usually give birth to litters of four or fewer each year.

LAGOMORPHS

Splitting Hares: Lagomorphs are divided into two families—the rabbits and hares, and the pikas. There's not so much variety in the lagomorph order as there is among the rodents. Lagomorphs all move by hopping or running, eat mostly grasses, stems, and bark, and have similarly shaped bodies covered with long, soft fur.

second set of incisors
(not continuously growing)

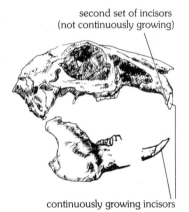

continuously growing incisors

Leaping Lagomorphs: It's easy to confuse rabbits with hares. Both are great jumpers, with long, strong hindlegs and fur-covered feet that give them a good grip on slippery surfaces. And they both have long, narrow ears and short, fluffy tails. But there are some major differences between hares and rabbits:

- *To Dig or Not to Dig:* Hares usually live in open areas and rely on running in zigzag patterns to escape predators. Slower-moving rabbits often dig burrows and scamper into their homes when threatened.
- *Hey, Baby:* Rabbits and hares also have different kinds of babies. Young hares are *precocial,* which means that they're born with hair and open eyes and can run around within a few minutes of birth. Newborn rabbits are *altricial*—they're hairless, helpless, and blind. (For more about precocial and altricial young, see "The Early Days" on pages 26 and 27 of *NatureScope: Amazing Mammals—Part I.)*

Mini-Haymakers: Weighing in at about a half pound (.2 kg), with small, rounded ears and a barely visible tail, a pika looks as if it's more closely related to a guinea pig than to a rabbit or hare. These "unconventional" lagomorphs live in parts of North America, eastern Europe, and Asia. They spend most of the day during the summer and fall collecting grasses, spreading them to dry in the sun, and then storing this hay for winter food.

Habitats for Hoppers

Make a rabbit and hare habitat mural.

Objectives:
Describe the habitats of cottontail rabbits, jackrabbits, and snowshoe hares. Discuss rabbit and hare adaptations.

Ages:
Primary

Materials:
- *three bedsheets or three pieces of mural paper*
- *pictures of a black-tailed jackrabbit, snowshoe hare, and cottontail rabbit*
- *pictures of a meadow, northern evergreen forest, and desert*
- *construction paper*
- *8½ × 11" pieces of drawing paper*
- *scissors*
- *glue*
- *markers*
- *Velcro fasteners*
- *cotton balls*

Subjects:
Science and Art

ave your kids make a habitat mural to learn where cottontails, jackrabbits, and snowshoe hares live. Here's how:

1. Copy and enlarge each of the outlines shown below onto a separate 8½ × 11" piece of paper. (Enlarge to the dimensions indicated for each drawing.) Then make enough copies of each outline for one-third of your group.

2. Divide the kids into three groups: the cottontails, the jackrabbits, and the snowshoe hares. Review the characteristics of these mammals using the background information on pages 45-46. Show the kids pictures of the animals and the different habitats they live in as you talk about each one. (cottontail—meadow; jackrabbit—desert; snowshoe hare—northern evergreen forest) Then pass out an outline and a piece of construction paper to each person. (Pass out brown construction paper for the jackrabbits and cottontails and white paper for the snowshoe hares.)

3. To make their outlines sturdier, have the kids glue them to the construction paper and let dry. (Tell the kids not to use too much glue or the edges of their cut-outs will curl.) Then have them cut out the shapes.

4. Pass out Velcro fasteners and have the kids glue one half of the fastener near the top of their cut-outs and let dry. *Note:* Velcro comes in two parts: One half is covered with hooks and the other half is covered with fuzzy hairs. Have all the kids glue the same side of the Velcro to their cut-outs.

5. Spread the mural paper (or sheets) on the floor and explain that each group will work together to make a different type of habitat mural. The cottontails can draw grasses, shrubs, and other meadow plants on their mural, or cut out shapes from green or brown construction paper. The jackrabbits can illustrate a rocky desert scattered with sagebrush and cactuses. And the snowshoe hares can make a winter forest scene by cutting out or drawing evergreen trees and gluing on cotton balls for snow.

6. After the kids finish their habitats, glue the free halves of the Velcro throughout the three habitats. Let the glue dry, then have the kids attach their mammals in the appropriate habitats.

Afterward, discuss how these rabbits and hares have special characteristics that help them live where they do. For example, snowshoe hares have brown fur in summer and white fur in winter. In summer, the brown fur helps them hide in vegetation. In winter, the white fur helps them blend in with snow. Try switching some of the snowshoe hares with the jackrabbits and cottontails to show how this winter camouflage works. You might also want to talk about how all rabbits and hares have special hopping hindlegs that help them escape from predators, how cottontails often hop into thick meadow foliage to hide, and how jackrabbits are adapted to desert life (see page 27 in *NatureScope—Discovering Deserts*).

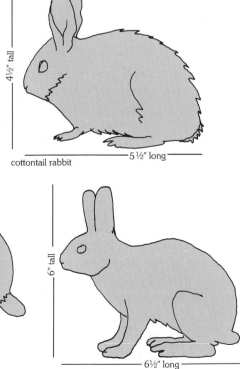

cottontail rabbit

4½" tall — 5½" long

black-tailed jackrabbit

8½" long — 8½" tall

snowshoe hare

6" tall — 6½" long

Cartoon Gnawers

Create a cartoon strip featuring a rodent or lagomorph.

Objectives:
Discuss anthropomorphism. Describe some characteristics of rodents and lagomorphs.

Ages:
Intermediate and Advanced

Materials:
- *copies of page 51*
- *picture of a mammal cartoon character*
- *examples of comic strips or cartoons that feature mammal characters*
- *crayons or colored pencils*
- *drawing paper and pencils*
- *rulers*
- *reference books*
- *tracing paper (optional)*

Subjects:
Science and Art

Bugs Bunny, Mickey Mouse, Rocky the Squirrel, and Spike the Porcupine are just a few of the cartoon characters inspired by rodents, rabbits, and hares. By creating their own cartoon characters, your kids can learn more about how these real mammals live.

by C. & S. Hart

PART 1: INTRODUCING THE CHARACTER

Begin the first part of the activity by showing the kids a mammal cartoon character. Ask them to describe what's not realistic about the character. (depending on the character—wears clothes, talks, has a job, has human feelings and personality)

Explain that when people give animals human feelings such as anger or happiness and have them speak, wear clothing, or do other things that people normally do, they are creating *anthropomorphic* characters. Ask the kids to name some more mammal cartoon or comic strip characters. (Snoopy, Marmaduke, Garfield, and so on) Then discuss the humanlike qualities and the realistic mammal characteristics of each of the cartoon characters named. Wrap up this part of the activity by asking the kids to bring in examples of mammal cartoons or comic strips the next time your group meets.

PART 2: DEVELOPING THE CHARACTER

Ask the kids these questions as you discuss the comics they collected:
- What do the comics have in common? (Something happens to the main character. Most try to be funny.)
- Are all the cartoons the same length? (They probably vary in length from one to eight frames.)
- What kinds of things are the mammal cartoon characters doing?
- Describe the personalities of the characters. How does the artist give the character a personality? (with the clothing the character wears, its expressions, the things it says and does)
- If any mammal information is presented, is it accurate? (Some comic strips may show where the mammal lives, the kinds of foods it eats, the sounds it makes, and so on.)

Next tell the kids that they will be developing their own cartoon characters based on facts about the real animals. Then pass out copies of page 51 to the group. Eight cartoon characters are illustrated on the page. Each is a type of rodent or lagomorph. The name of each character appears under the picture. Go over the page and talk about the special mammal characteristics that are illustrated and humanized. For example, "Speedy Jackrabbit" is wearing sneakers and running shorts to show that it is a speedy runner. (You may also want to go over the general characteristics of rodents and lagomorphs. For background information, see pages 45–46.)

Explain that each child should choose one character to use as the subject of a cartoon strip. Tell the kids that their cartoons should include some natural history information about their mammals, as well as develop their character's personality. Give the kids research time to find out what their mammals eat, where they live, if they build a nest or shelter, what kind of social group (if any) they live in, and other interesting facts.

After the kids have gathered their information, have them think of ways to present the information in a cartoon strip. They can illustrate the backgrounds of their cartoons to show the type of habitat their mammal lives in, or show interactions between the cartoon characters and other animals that live in the same habitat. They can set up situations in the cartoons that show how their mammals stay alive in the wild. (You may want to give younger kids story suggestions from the list on the right to get them started.)

Pass out pencils, rulers, drawing paper, and crayons or colored pencils. Then have the kids pick the character or characters on page 51 they want to use. They can add their own characters, adapt the pictures, change the names, or do whatever they want to create their cartoons. (You can have them trace the figures, or draw the characters freehand, changing the characters' positions in each frame to fit their storyline.) Tell the kids to use rulers to draw the frames of the cartoon strips. After everyone is finished, share the cartoons with the group.

Suggested story lines:

- black-tailed prairie dog spots ferret entering "town"
- flying squirrel practices landing techniques
- woodrat steals shiny items from miners
- pocket gopher builds new tunnel
- jackrabbit enters running race
- pika makes hay for the upcoming winter
- beaver "engineers" new dam with the help of its family
- porcupine is threatened by a hungry bobcat

The Great Rodent Expedition

Create journal entries to record a worldwide rodent discovery expedition.

Objective:
Give an example of a rodent and describe the geographic region where it lives and how it is adapted to that habitat.

Ages:
Advanced

Materials:
- *copies of page 52*
- *reference books*
- *crayons or markers*
- *writing paper*
- *construction paper*
- *stapler*

Subjects:
Science, Geography, and Creative Writing

September 10. Early this morning, as we rounded a bend in the river, we saw some incredible beasts. They were fairly large—each weighing around one hundred pounds—and they were covered with coarse yellowish brown fur. Their eyes were small and piglike, and their noses were long and blunt. There were at least a dozen of them sunning on the banks of the river. As we came closer, they plunged into the water and swam swiftly away—more like fish than beasts! One of our hunters fired and killed one of the creatures. We feasted on its flesh that evening—most tasty!

A journal entry like this might have been written by the first explorer to see a capybara, the world's largest rodent. Your kids, by writing their own explorer journals, can learn about a variety of "gnawers" around the world, as well as review world geography.

Begin the activity by passing out copies of page 52. Explain that ten animals have been drawn on the map in the areas where they live. (In some cases, these mammals are also found in other areas around the world.) Tell the kids to imagine that they are explorers on an early scientific expedition, sailing around the world in search of new kinds of animals.

Each entry in their journals should describe an encounter with one of the rodents on the map. (Read the opening paragraph of this activity as an example of a journal entry.) Tell the kids to put themselves in the place of someone who has never before seen these animals. What would they notice first? Here are some ideas for what their entries might include:

- what the rodent looks like
- the kind of habitat where it lives— grassy plains, forests, near water, and so on
- what it eats
- whether it lives alone or with other animals
- any unique or interesting behaviors

(continued next page)

Len Rue, Jr. beaver

The kids can also write about how these animals affected the people that lived in these areas. (Some rodents were raised for food and fur and others became pets. Some transmitted deadly diseases and destroyed crops and many were purposefully or accidentally introduced to new areas by earlier explorers. For historical notes about these animals, see the background information below.)

The kids can also include some geographical notes in their entries. Have them use reference books to find out what countries these animals live in and what the areas look like. They should also specify the direction (north, south, east, or west) they are traveling in and the countries or oceans they cross as they make their expeditions. They can illustrate their routes by drawing colorful arrows on their maps.

After the kids have written journal entries describing all the rodents on the map, have them make journal covers by folding pieces of construction paper in half. They can decorate their covers and color their maps and rodent drawings. Have them staple their papers together inside the covers. Then ask for volunteers to read a few entries and see if the rest of the group can match each one with the rodent being described.

CAPYBARA
- largest living rodent (77 to 146 lbs [35 to 66 kg])
- source of meat and skin since 16th century
- lives in grasslands near rivers and streams
- good swimmer—has slightly webbed feet and is able to stay underwater for up to five minutes
- feeds on grasses that grow near water
- lives in small groups

BEAVER
- considered sacred by some native North Americans
- demand for its fur helped open up the American West
- by the 1840's, had been trapped nearly to extinction
- always lives near water
- builds dams and lodges
- lives in family groups

ROOF OR BLACK RAT
- native to India, but now found on every continent except Antarctica
- transported to other countries by ships
- can carry fleas infected with plague, the disease that killed one-fourth of Europe's population in the 14th century
- a pest to farmers—eats and damages crops

SPRINGHARE
- not a hare, but a rodent
- major source of meat and skin for African Bushmen
- lives in grassy areas and feeds on grass
- has powerful hind feet—can leap 10-13 ft (3-4 m) to escape predators
- digs burrows
- when not in its burrow, travels in small groups

GUINEA PIG
- raised by Incas for meat
- its flesh tastes like pork
- makes a variety of squeaks, chirps, and squeals
- no longer found in the wild (now raised in captivity for its meat and has become a popular pet and laboratory animal)

GIANT FLYING SQUIRREL
- hunted for its meat by aborigines living in Taiwan
- considered a pest of fruit crops
- lives in mountain forests
- eats fruit and other plant parts
- usually lives in pairs
- can glide up to 1300 ft (390 m)

HAMSTER
- originally found only in Middle East (now a common worldwide pet and laboratory animal)
- carries food in large cheek pouches
- eats mostly seeds and other plant parts
- lives alone

GERBIL
- native to Mongolia (now a common worldwide pet)
- adapted to living in desert areas—digs burrows to stay cool; needs very little water
- lives in large groups

EDIBLE OR FAT DORMOUSE
- raised by ancient Romans for food
- hibernates for several months
- has a long bushy tail that can come off if grabbed by a predator
- eats fruit, nuts, seeds
- lives in small groups
- lives in forests

HOUSE MOUSE
- native to the Old World
- can adapt to a wide range of habitats and eats many types of food
- "stowed away" on ships and was transported worldwide
- a serious pest—eats crops and damages homes
- populations can increase dramatically

Fearless Fran the
Flying Squirrel

Peter the Pika

Hawkeye
the Pocket Gopher

Speedy the Jackrabbit

Petula
the Black-tailed
Prairie Dog

Bucky the Beaver

Perry the Porcupine

Woody the Woodrat

THE GREAT RODENT EXPEDITION

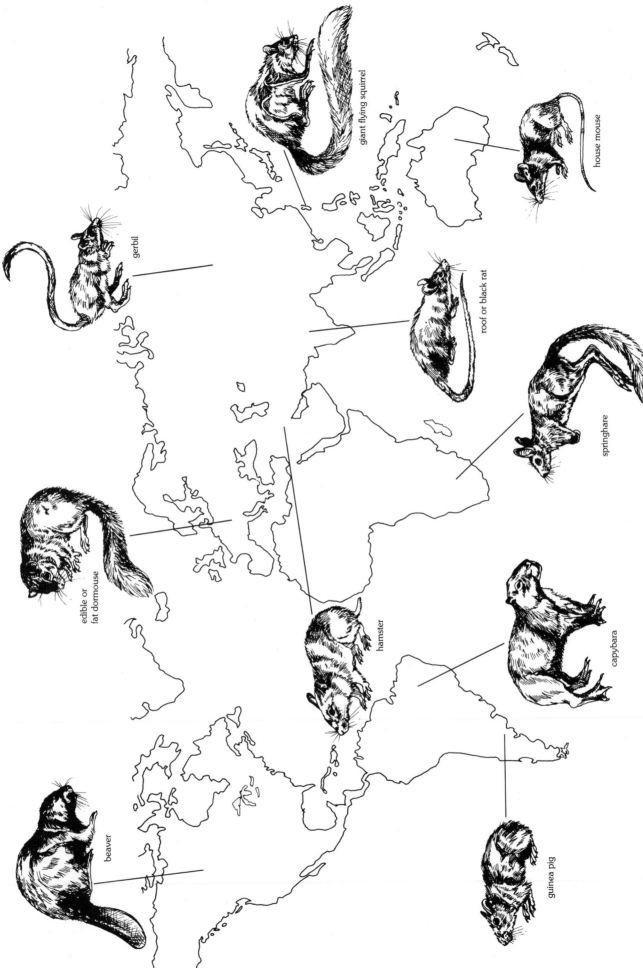

giant flying squirrel

house mouse

gerbil

roof or black rat

springhare

edible or
fat dormouse

hamster

capybara

beaver

guinea pig

THE INSECT EATERS

ll insectivores have one thing in common—they're small! None is larger than a rabbit and some are so tiny they weigh less than a dime. In this chapter we'll take a look at the habits of this group of miniature mammals, which includes the moles, shrews, hedgehogs, tenrecs, and others, and find out what makes the insectivores unique.

MEET THE INSECTIVORES

Besides being small, most insectivores are nocturnal and somewhat secretive—traits that make these mammals tough to study and hard to see in the wild. But if a small, furry body should scurry by, look to see if it has a sharp, pointed nose, tiny ears, and small or partially hidden eyes. If it does, chances are it's an insectivore. Most insectivores also have tiny brains and primitive teeth, and, as their name indicates, feed on insects. But they also eat other small creatures, including worms, spiders, fish, frogs, lizards, and mice, as well as carrion. Here's a quick run-down on who's who among the insectivores:

Shrews: These aggressive little mammals look like miniature mice with long, pointed noses and very tiny eyes that are often hidden by fur. Instead of relying on sight to find food, shrews rely on their keen senses of smell and hearing. Some even have a crude ability to echolocate, using high-pitched, clicking sounds. (For more about echolocation, see "Bouncing Off the Walls" on page 34.)

Shrews also have a very high metabolic rate and must eat almost constantly, day and night, to avoid starving. They attack insects, worms, and other invertebrates, as well as other shrews, mice, and voles. They also feed on carrion and on seeds, nuts, and other plant material.

One type of shrew—the short-tailed shrew—is one of the few mammals that use poison to help them get a meal. These North American shrews have nerve poison in their saliva, which can paralyze and kill mice and other small prey.

Although most shrews live only on land, a few are aquatic or partially aquatic and feed on aquatic insects, crustaceans, and other water creatures.

(continued next page)

shrew

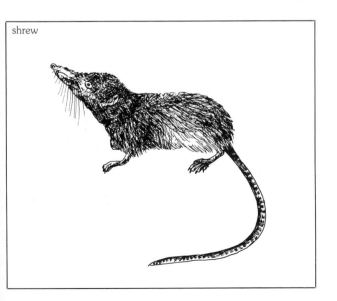

hedgehog

mole

tenrec

Moles: Moles and most mole relatives are burrowers and are well equipped for a subterranean life. They have powerful front feet that seem to grow straight out from their shoulders. And at the end of each foot are strong claws well suited for digging. Moles also have velvety, thick fur that lies flat against their skin. And their bodies are tapered at both ends for easy tunneling.

As moles dig, they look as if they are swimming through the soil. They twist their bodies forward, pressing loose dirt against the sides of their tunnels with their feet. Occasionally moles tunnel to the surface and deposit soil there, creating molehills. Some aquatic species have passages that end underwater in ponds or streams.

Most moles rely on a super sense of touch to find food. Many have whiskers on their faces and tails, as well as sensitive bumps on their snouts. The starnose mole has a super-sensitive snout and is the weirdest-looking mole of all—it has 22 fleshy feelers on the end of its snout that wave in all directions to help it find food.

There are about 25 kinds of moles that live in forests and fields and along riverbanks in parts of Europe, Asia, and North America. There are also molelike mammals in Africa (called golden moles for their sandy-colored, sometimes iridescent fur) that live in desert and savannah areas.

Hedgehogs: These spiny, nocturnal mammals are probably the best-liked insectivores in the world. In many parts of Europe and Asia, people feed them at night and sometimes keep them as pets to help control insect pests.

Hedgehogs are covered with thousands of sharp, stiff spines, giving them a roly-poly, pincushion appearance. As additional protection, many hedgehogs can curl into a ball, tucking their head and legs out of sight. Only a few predators, such as badgers and foxes, can pry open a prickly hedgehog ball.

Hedgehogs often catch and eat things that other animals avoid, such as bees, wasps, and poisonous snakes. And many seem to be immune to certain animal poisons and aren't usually affected if they do get bitten or stung. Hedgehogs also feed on other insects, eggs, frogs, baby mice, lizards, and carrion.

Tenrecs: "Strange" and "diverse" are the best words to describe tenrecs. Some look like hedgehogs, with spine-covered bodies. Others look more like shrews, moles, or mice. Some are tiny and have ratlike tails; others are as big as rabbits and have tiny tails. Some can climb, some can run, some can jump, and some can dig.

As different as they all are, most tenrecs do share some common traits, such as poor eyesight, relatively small brains, and a home on Madagascar. And like other insectivores, they feed on insects, earthworms, mice, and lizards.

Tenrecs often have large litters. One type of tenrec holds the placental mammalian record for the most offspring produced in one litter—over 25!

Little Starnose

Listen to a story about a starnose mole and make a mole nose out of cardboard and construction paper.

Objective:
Describe how a starnose mole finds food, escapes from enemies, and is adapted to life underground.

Ages:
Primary

Materials:
- *story on page 56*
- *cardboard egg cartons*
- *pink construction paper*
- *glue*
- *scissors*
- *yarn*
- *pictures of moles*
- *paper punch*

Subject:
Science

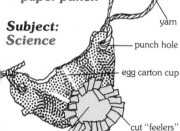

yarn
punch hole
egg carton cup
cut "feelers"
pink construction paper

This activity will introduce your kids to one of the strangest-looking animals in the world—the starnose mole. Start off the activity by asking if anyone has ever seen a mole. Then ask if anyone has seen a molehill or tunnel. Explain that most people never see moles because these animals live underground. But as moles tunnel underground, using their strong front legs to dig, they sometimes make raised tunnels and piles of dirt aboveground.

Show the children pictures of common moles, including the starnose mole. (For suggestions of where to get mole pictures, see page 91.) Point out the sharp digging claws, strong front legs, and smooth fur. Ask the kids what they think the fleshy feelers on the starnose mole's nose are used for. Then tell them they will find out when you read them a story about a starnose mole named Little Starnose. And as you read the story, have the children act out certain words as they hear them. Here are some suggestions for movements you can have them make each time they hear the word or words marked in bold type below:

- **starnose or starnose mole**—Make "feelers" by placing a hand on each side of nose with fingers outstretched and thumbs facing each other. Wiggle fingers.
- **footsteps**—Stomp feet three times.
- **earthworm**—Hold out index finger and bend it back and forth.
- **swim, swam, or swimming**— Pretend to swim.

Practice each movement several times, then read the story and see if the kids can remember what to do when. (In the story, the "movement" words are shown in italics.) Afterward talk about the habits of the starnose mole and how it uses its fleshy feelers to help it find food.

Then pass out egg cartons, scissors, glue, construction paper, and yarn and have each person make his or her own starnose mole nose. Here's how:

1. Cut out one cup of a cardboard egg carton (see diagram).
2. Cut out a circle from pink construction paper.
3. Glue the circle to the flat part of the egg carton and let dry. Then cut "fleshy feelers" out of the circle, as shown. Bend up every other feeler to make the nose look more like that of a starnose mole and less like that of a pig.
4. Punch a hole in each side of the nose and attach yarn so the kids can wear their noses.

(continued next page)

Luise Woelflein

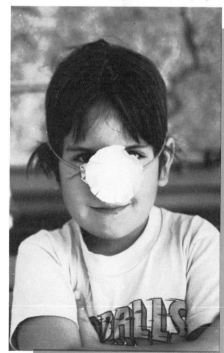

LITTLE STARNOSE

Adapted from a story by Tom Monser

Little *Starnose* was a *starnose mole*. He was a bit funny-looking, as moles go. On the end of his pointed nose were *22 feelers*. The feelers helped *Starnose* search for food as he snuffled along underground. Now his feelers were wiggling like crazy as *Starnose* dug through the soft dirt. His strong front legs pushed the dirt behind him as he dug another tunnel in the Martins' backyard. On the surface, the dirt formed a small mound.

Footsteps on the ground above him warned Little *Starnose* that something was coming. He stopped digging to listen. Of course, *Starnose* didn't know that there were people up there. And he couldn't hear, or know, what they were saying about him.

"Just look at these molehills all over the place!" exclaimed Mrs. Martin. "That mole is making a real mess back here by our pond. Oh, well. We can't do anything about it this evening. Let's go see if dinner is ready."

Jimmy Martin could tell that his mother wasn't happy about the mole problem. She was very proud of her pretty yard. But Jimmy thought the molehills looked neat. They looked like little mountains to him. He wished that he could see the little mountain-maker someday.

A few inches below Jimmy's feet sat *Starnose*, the mountain-maker. The mole felt the ground shake a little as Mrs. Martin and Jimmy walked away. *Starnose* started to dig a deeper, safer tunnel. But then he stopped digging again. He was hungry. Fat *earthworms* would make a nice mole meal!

Like other moles, *Starnose* rarely came aboveground. It was too dangerous up there. Owls, foxes, weasels, or other hungry animals could catch him. But sometimes rain drove many *earthworms* to the surface. Then hungry *Starnose* dared to go aboveground. This was one of those times.

Starnose poked his funny snout out of the ground. He sniffed the air, then waddled away from his tunnel. He began hunting for food. But while Little *Starnose* was hunting for *earthworms,* a hungry weasel was hunting for him. Would *Starnose* sense that an enemy was coming in time for him to escape?

He did! *Starnose* dived back into his tunnel. He raced along underground as fast as he could go. The weasel paused at the opening of the tunnel. She sniffed to catch *Starnose's* scent. Then she slipped down into the tunnel after him.

Luckily for *Starnose,* he was in a tunnel that ended right at the edge of the

Martins' pond. *Splash!* He dived into the water and *swam* quickly away. When the weasel got to the end of that tunnel, Little *Starnose* was gone. She would have to look elsewhere for something to eat.

Little *Starnose* was a very good *swimmer*. And now that he was in the pond, he searched for something to eat. His funny nose wiggled this way and that. Soon he caught a minnow and *swam* back to the edge of the pond. He scooted up onto the bank and stopped. There sat Jimmy Martin.

After dinner, Jimmy had been sitting by the pond watching frogs. He had heard the tiny splash as *Starnose* plopped into the pond. Jimmy watched the small, dark, furry animal *swimming*. He watched as it climbed up the pond's bank. And he watched the mole's funny nose wiggle as the mole watched him. Jimmy laughed out loud at the mole's wiggly nose.

Little *Starnose* scurried back into his tunnel. He was full and safe once more. Jimmy was happy as he walked back to his house. He had seen the little mountain-maker that lived in his backyard.

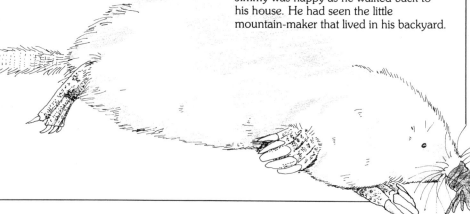

You and a Shrew

Fill in a chart that compares humans to shrews.

Objectives:
Compare size, physiology, and other characteristics of shrews and humans. Take pulse rates and breathing rates.

Ages:
Intermediate and Advanced

How are humans different from tiny, insect-eating shrews? In this activity your group will get a chance to find out by comparing a representative shrew—the pygmy shrew—to themselves.

Before starting the activity, trace the human shape drawn in the margin eight times on a piece of paper and put a number (from 1 to 8) beside each one. Then make enough copies of the page for the group.

Now ask the kids to describe what a shrew is. Write the descriptive words or phrases on a chalkboard or large piece of

easel paper. Then show the kids pictures of common shrews. Point out the tiny eyes, long pointed snouts, and thick fur. Explain that like humans, shrews are warm-blooded, give birth to live young, and nurse their young with milk—characteristics that are typical of almost all mammals. Both shrews and humans are also omnivorous. But in many ways, shrews are very different from humans.

Divide the group into pairs and pass out copies of page 58 and the page of blank human shapes. Tell each team that they will have to find a human fact that corresponds to each shrew fact. Point out that part of each shrew fact is italicized. They

Materials:
- *watch or clock that records seconds*
- *copies of page 58*
- *paper*
- *pen or pencil*
- *scissors (optional)*
- *construction paper*
- *chalkboard or easel paper*
- *food scale*
- *scale that records body weight*
- *pictures of shrews*

Subject:
Science

will need to rewrite the fact and fill in the correct number, word, or phrase in the human shape of the same number. For example, shrew number 1 says "I weigh *less than a penny."* Tell the kids they will need to weigh themselves and write this fact in human shape number 1. (See "Human Facts" at the end of the activity for some average characteristics of adults and kids.)

Some of the facts are harder to find than others. For example, give the kids the answer to number 4 (shrews can starve to death in six hours, but it would take a human about 20 to 30 days) and any others you think are tricky. The kids should be able to figure out most of the answers themselves. For example, to find out how many times they breathe a minute, have one of the kids in each pair count while his or her partner breathes. Then have them switch roles. Also show the kids how to take their pulse rate. Have them take a resting pulse first, then have them do twenty jumping jacks and take their pulse again. To find how much food they eat in a day, have them weigh their food on a food scale. (If it's too much trouble to weigh breakfast, lunch, and dinner, just have them weigh their lunch and multiply by three to get an approximate figure for the day.) Then show them how to figure out what percentage of their body weight this is.

Afterward go over the human facts that the kids came up with and talk about the differences between shrews and humans. Explain that shrews have a very high metabolic rate, which means that their heart rate, breathing rate, and other body functions are very fast compared to those of humans. Shrews need to eat almost constantly to stay alive because they burn up their food energy almost immediately. This high metabolic rate is the reason that shrews usually live only a year or two. Their bodies just burn themselves out!

HUMAN FACTS

1. I weigh *about 70 pounds.*
2. Most people are *not colorblind.*
3. I breathe *about 20* times a minute.
4. People starve to death in *about 20 to 30 days.*
5. My heart beats *about 80* times a minute when I'm resting and *about 120* times a minute when I'm very active.
6. I will probably live *about 70 or more years.*
7. I am *about 54 inches (1.4 m) tall.*
8. I eat *less than one-fourteenth of* my weight in food each day.

SHREW FACTS

1. I weigh *less than a penny.*
2. I am *colorblind.*
3. I breathe *about 850* times a minute.
4. I can starve to death in *about 6 hours.*
5. My heart beats *about 600* times a minute when I'm resting and *about 800* times a minute when I'm active.
6. I will probably live *about a year.*
7. I am *about 3 inches (7.5 cm) long.*
8. I eat *about one and one half times* my weight in food each day.

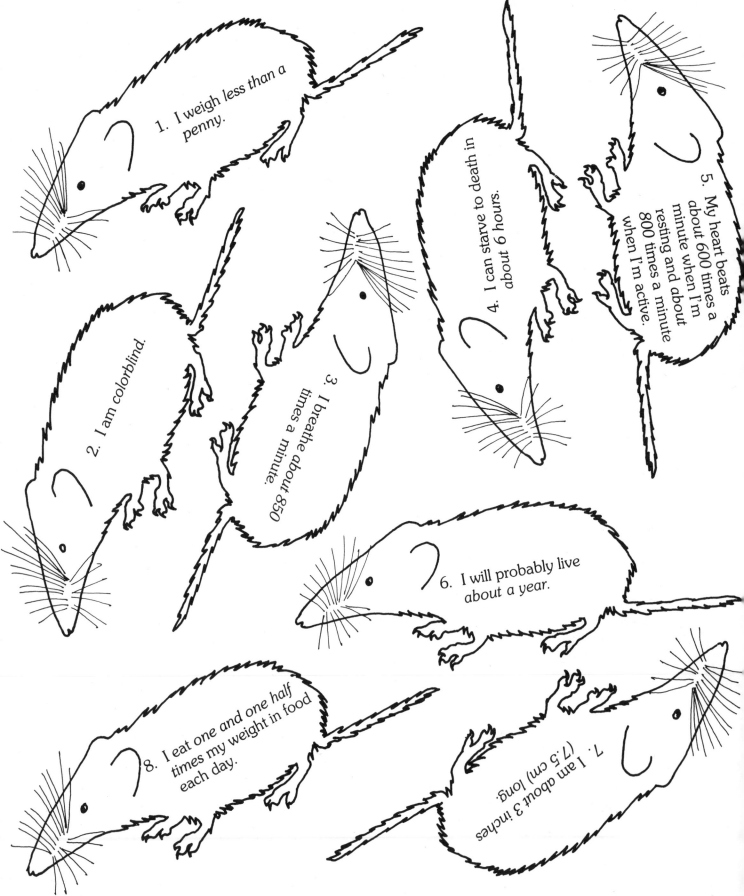

1. I weigh less than a penny.

2. I am colorblind.

3. I breathe about 850 times a minute.

4. I can starve to death in about 6 hours.

5. My heart beats about 600 times a minute when I'm resting and about 800 times a minute when I'm active.

6. I will probably live about a year.

7. I am about 3 inches (7.5 cm) long.

8. I eat one and one half times my weight in food each day.

MAMMALS OF THE SEA

e'd have to go back more than 50 million years to see some of the sea mammals' earliest ancestors. But we'd have to look for them on land! These land-dwelling predecessors of modern sea mammals gradually moved into the sea. And over the years they developed some amazing adaptations that helped them meet the challenges of a watery environment.

ADAPTING TO THE DEEP

Today there are more than a hundred species of sea mammals, and they're divided into three groups: the whales, dolphins, and porpoises (known as *cetaceans*); the seals, sea lions, and walruses (*pinnipeds*); and the dugongs and manatees (*sirenians*). Despite the fact that they're all called *sea* mammals, at least one species in each of these groups lives in freshwater rivers or lakes.

Cetaceans, pinnipeds, and sirenians aren't related to one another—each, in fact, evolved from a separate group of land animals. But they do have some similar adaptations to underwater life. Here's a look at a few of these adaptations:

Streamlined Swimmers: Torpedo-shaped bodies help marine mammals move through the water with as little resistance as possible. And some of these mammals, such as many species of seals, have dense, sleek fur that also helps to minimize drag. But whales and some other sea mammals have taken the concept of streamlining a step farther: They've completely lost the fur coats of their ancestors, leaving only a layer of smooth skin for water to rush past as they swim.

Blubbery Bodies: Sea mammals, like all mammals, are warm-blooded and must maintain a constant internal body temperature. One feature that keeps these animals from losing too much heat to chilly ocean waters is a layer of fat just under the skin. This insulating layer, called *blubber,* varies in thickness from one species to the next. In some seals, it may be only a few inches thick. (A dense fur coat makes up for the thin layer of blubber.) But the blubber layer of many whales can be thicker than one foot (30 cm)!

A Fitting Physiology: When you think about it, it's pretty amazing that some mammals have actually managed to make the water a permanent home. Mammals, after all, must breathe air—they don't have gills for extracting oxygen from water as fish and other water animals do. This means that sea mammals must come up to the water's surface from time to time to breathe.

But many sea mammals are able to spend a lot of time far below the water's surface. They dive to search for food, avoid enemies, and so on—and some of them can stay down for long periods of time. Sperm whales, for example, can stay under the surface for an hour and fifteen minutes without coming up for air!

Because they can hold their breath for so long, marine mammals' systems are often deprived of a fresh flow of oxygen for quite a while. How, then, does a sea mammal keep its heart and other muscles and body parts running smoothly while it's diving? The answer has to do with some special physiological adaptations. For example, sea mammals can store much more oxygen in their muscles than land mammals can, and their blood contains many more oxygen-carrying red blood cells. Also, most of a diving sea mammal's blood goes primarily to its heart and brain, skipping the skin and other "less important" organs altogether. And as it dives, its heart rate slows down, helping to conserve oxygen. *(continued next page)*

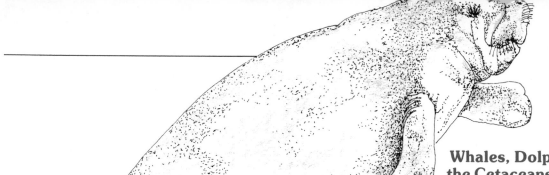

manatee

Below is a quick look at each of the three groups of sea mammals:

Whales, Dolphins, and Porpoises—the Cetaceans: This group includes the largest animals ever to live on earth. (Scientists think that not even the biggest dinosaurs were as big as the blue whale.) But not all cetaceans are huge. The harbor porpoise, for example, grows to be only about five feet (1.5 m) long. Scientists have divided the cetaceans into two main sub-groups, based on the animals' feeding habits. The largest sub-group—which includes, among others, bottlenose dolphins, belugas, and orcas (killer whales)—are known as the *toothed whales.* Most of these mammals prey on fish, birds, seals, or other animals, and many use echolocation to help them find their prey. (For more about echolocation, see "Bouncing Off the Walls" on page 34.) And not surprisingly, most toothed whales are equipped with a mouthful of teeth.

Baleen whales, on the other hand, don't have any teeth. Fish make up part of their diet, but they get most of their nourishment from tiny crustaceans and other animals that are known collectively as plankton. They feed by taking in huge amounts of water, then pushing the water through the gigantic plates, called *baleen,* that line their mouths. The water filters back into the ocean, but the plankton and other food are trapped by the baleen. Most of the largest whales, such as blues, grays, and humpbacks, are baleen whales.

A few more cetacean facts: All cetaceans breathe through one or two *blowholes* (nostrils) on the tops of their heads. And most live and travel together in groups. Cetaceans have a great capacity for communication, and they often "talk" to one another by making complex clicking, moaning, and whistling sounds.

Seals and Walruses—the Pinnipeds: These animals are the "land lovers" among the three groups of sea mammals. Whereas sirenians (see below) and cetaceans are pretty much water bound all of their lives, the pinnipeds often climb onto ice floes or spend time on beaches. During the breeding season, in fact, certain beaches are inundated with pinnipeds—sometimes more than a hundred thousand of them on a single beach!

Like the toothed whales, most pinnipeds have teeth that are adapted for catching fish, squid, birds, and other animals. (Some also use echolocation to help them hunt, just as many of the whales do.) But the teeth of some species are highly specialized. Walruses, for example, use their long canine teeth, or *tusks,* to chop breathing holes in the ice, to haul themselves out of the water, and as a display to show one another who's boss.

Dugongs and Manatees—the Sirenians: These calm, slow-moving sea mammals are strict herbivores, and their feeding habits have earned them the nickname of "sea cow." In some areas these aquatic "cows" have helped people by eating their way through plant-clogged water highways.

Plants are hard on teeth, and they're difficult to digest. But sirenians have some special adaptations for dealing with these problems. For example, new teeth move in from the backs of manatees' jaws to take the place of teeth that are worn out. (No other sea mammal can replace its teeth in this way.) And incredibly long intestines—more than 150 feet (45 m) in some sirenians—help in the breakdown of the tough plant fibers that these underwater grazers feed on.

Wonderful Whales!

Sing a song about whales and draw a blue whale to scale on blacktop.

Objectives:
Name several differences between fish and whales. Describe several features of whales and explain how these features help whales live in the ocean. State several facts about blue whales.

Ages:
Primary and Intermediate

Materials:
- *pictures of fish and whales*
- *guitar or piano (optional)*
- *recording of humpback whale songs (optional)*
- *chalk*
- *measuring tape or yardstick*
- *record or tape player*

Subjects:
Science and Music

Here are a couple of activities that will get your kids thinking, talking, and singing about whales.

WHALE MUSIC

Start this activity by leading a brief discussion about whales in general. Explain that for many years people thought whales were huge fish. But scientists eventually discovered that these animals are mammals, just as people are. Unlike most fish, they're warm-blooded, bear live young, nurse their young with milk from their bodies, and must come up to the water's surface to breathe. (For more about the characteristics of mammals, see pages 3-5 of *NatureScope: Amazing Mammals—Part I.* And for information on the characteristics of fish and other non-mammals, and the ways they differ from mammals, see "The Vertebrate Grab Game" on page 13 of *Amazing Mammals—Part I.*)

As you show the kids pictures of whales and fish, explain that another difference between the two kinds of animals has to do with the way they swim. Fish swim by moving their tails from side to side. Whales, on the other hand, move their tails, or *flukes,* up and down. Point to the tails in the pictures of both animals so the kids can see that each of them is built for moving in a certain way.

Here are a few more whale facts you can cover:
- A whale's side fins, called *flippers,* help the animal steer. (Point to the flippers in a picture of a whale.)
- A thick layer of fat, called *blubber,* keeps whales warm in the chilly ocean waters where they live. (For more about blubber, see page 59.)
- Whales breathe through one or two *blowholes* located on the top of their heads. Show the kids pictures of a whale spouting. Explain that when a whale does this, it's exhaling. The misty spray that comes out is the whale's breath. It changes to fine droplets of water when it hits the cool air, just as our own breath does when it's cold outside.

Now have the kids pretend that they're whales as they march around in a circle, sing the song shown below, and perform the motions that go with each verse. (Have them sing to the tune of "The Farmer in the Dell.") *(continued next page)*

Luise Woelflein

VERSES

1. My flukes move up and down,
   My flukes move up and down,
   Heigh-ho the whale-oh,
   My flukes move up and down.

2. My flippers help me steer, etc.

3. My blubber keeps me warm, etc.

4. My blowhole helps me breathe, etc.

MOTIONS

1. Place hands side by side, with palms up, on your backside (where a tail would be). Move them up and down.

2. Hold arms straight, slightly up from sides, and bend your body this way and that.

3. Wrap your arms across your chest and give yourself a hug.

4. Make a fist and place it on top of your head. Exhale loudly after the first, second, and fourth phrases in the verse.

After the kids sing about being a whale, you might want to have them listen to some real whale songs. (See the end of the activity for some suggestions of whale records you can play.) Explain that many kinds of whales make sounds, but one species—the humpback whale—sings long, complicated songs. Show the kids some pictures of humpbacks. (For several good pictures and a lot of information about these whales, see "A Whale of a Whale" on pages 27-32 of *Ranger Rick,* October 1984.)

Many scientists think that only male humpbacks sing, and that they do it to attract a mate. But nobody really knows for sure. One thing researchers do know, though, is that all of the singers in a particular area sing the same song. And the songs seem to change quite a bit from one year to the next.

DRAW A WHALE TO SCALE

Almost everyone is impressed with the sizes of whales. Try this short outdoor activity to help your kids visualize just how big the biggest species is.

Before the kids arrive on the day of the activity, measure off 100 feet (30 m) on a blacktop play area or parking lot. Then use chalk to draw the shape of a blue whale (see left) within that space so that it fills up the entire length. (Older kids might be able to draw the whale themselves.)

When you're ready to start the activity, show the kids a picture of a blue whale. Explain that these mammals are probably the largest animals *ever* to live. The biggest ones may get to be 100 feet (30 m) long and may weigh more than 80 tons (72 t). That's longer than three school buses parked end to end and heavier than 11 African elephants! Most scientists think that not even the largest dinosaurs got to be this big.

Now take the kids outside and lead them on a "tour" of the blue whale you drew. Have them walk inside the whale from head to tail so they can see how little of the whale the entire group fills up.

If you're working with older kids, you might also want to try letting one of the kids lie down along the length of the whale (at either the head or fluke end). Mark that person's length on the blacktop. Then give the kids measuring tape or a yardstick so they can figure out how many times longer the whale is than that person.

To wrap up the activity, ask the kids what they think whales this size might eat. Explain that, surprisingly enough, most of a blue whale's diet is made up of small shrimplike crustaceans called *krill*. During the winter blue whales don't eat much, but during other times of the year they eat incredible amounts of food. A single blue whale can eat as much as eight tons (7.2 t) of krill each day!

WHALE RECORDS

- "Songs of the Humpback Whale"
- "Deep Voices: The Second Whale Record" includes vocalizations of right and blue whales in addition to humpbacks.
- "Ocean of Song: Whale Voices" includes vocalizations of orcas (killer whales) in addition to humpbacks.
- "Callings" includes music by Paul Winter, with vocalizations of 15 different sea mammals incorporated into the music.

Some record stores and public libraries carry these records. You can also order them from Carolina Biological Supply Company, 2700 York Rd., Burlington, NC 27215.

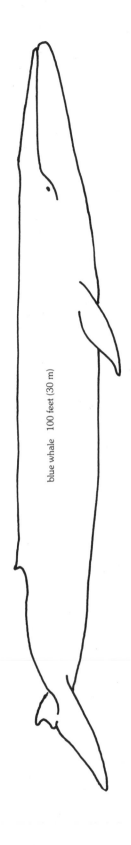

blue whale 100 feet (30 m)

Adopt a Sea Mammal

Become the adoptive "parents" of a sea mammal.

Objective:
Describe what an animal adoption program is and explain how such a program helps the animals involved.

Ages:
Primary, Intermediate, and Advanced

Subject:
Science

ZOOS AND AQUARIUMS
(*Note:* We've listed the sea mammals available for adoption in parentheses. Many other kinds of adoptable animals are also available.)

A.D.O.P.T
The Lincoln Park Zoological Society
2200 N. Cannon Dr.
Chicago, IL 60614
(312) 935-6700
(California sea lion, harbor seal)

ADOPT
The Philadelphia Zoo
34th St. and Girard Ave.
Philadelphia, PA 19104
(215) 243-1100, ext. 232
(harbor seal)

Adopt an Animal
San Francisco Zoological Society
Sloat Blvd. at the Pacific Ocean
San Francisco, CA 94132
(415) 753-7061
(California sea lion, harbor seal)

Adopt an Audubon Animal
Audubon Zoological Garden
P.O. Box 4327
New Orleans, LA 70178-9986
(504) 565-3006, ext. 543
(California sea lion)

Proud Parent Program
New England Aquarium
Central Wharf
Boston, MA 02110-3309
(617) 973-5294
(Bottle-nosed dolphin, California sea lion, harbor seal, right whale)

OTHER ORGANIZATIONS
Save the Manatee Club
1101 Audubon Way
Maitland, FL 32751
(800) 432-5646

Orca Adoption Program
Whale Museum
P.O. Box 945
Friday Harbor, WA 98250
(206) 378-4710

Whale Adoption Project
643 N. Falmouth Hwy., Box 388
North Falmouth, MA 02556
(508) 564-9980

I magine being the parent of a 40-ton (36-t) child. Or being the parent of someone who can eat the equivalent of 15 percent of his or her body weight in salad every day! "Kids" like these are up for adoption, and you and your group can be their proud "parents." The Whale Adoption Project has plenty of adoptable 40-ton-plus humpback whales. And the Save the Manatee Club offers more than twenty "ravenous" manatees. Many zoos and aquariums across the country also have adoption programs, and several of them feature sea mammals in addition to other kinds of animals.

The costs of adoption are often very inexpensive. For a minimum of ten dollars, for example, school groups or individual kids can adopt an endangered

Missoulian, November 1984

humpback whale through the Whale Adoption Project. And they can choose the whale from a list which includes the names of 70 whales and a little information about each one. Smoke, it reports, is a wanderer. And Patches entertains the crews of whalewatching boats with his breaching and flipper-slapping displays.

After sending in their adoption fee to the Whale Adoption Project, adoptive parents receive an adoption certificate of the whale of their choosing and a photograph of the animal. They also receive a quarterly publication called *Whalewatch* that discusses which whales have been sighted recently and how conservationists are working for the survival of humpbacks.

Ten dollars can also make your group the proud parents of an endangered manatee. Like the Whale Adoption Project, the Save the Manatee Club sends adoptive parents an adoption certificate, a photo of the adopted animal, and a newsletter containing articles about the animals and how they're being helped. Adoption fees for both the manatee and humpback programs contribute to scientific research, public awareness programs, and projects that help to ensure the animals' survival.

Adoption fees for zoos and aquariums, which also usually last for a year, are often higher than the manatee and whale projects. (These fees cover the costs of feeding and caring for the animals or of renovating their housing.) But some zoo programs have special rates which allow you to buy a share in the animal of your choice. Most zoos send adoptive parents (and shareholders) an adoption certificate, and many send other materials too (bumper stickers, decals, notes about the adopted animal, and so on). Some zoos also sponsor a special party or picnic for "parents."

You can have each person in your group bring in money for their special animal, or you can have them raise the money for the adoption fees themselves. (How about a "whale of a bake sale"?) In the left margin are just a few of the organizations that offer adoptable sea mammals.

Sea Mammal Sleuths

Match clues to the sea mammals they go with.

Objective:
Give examples of several different sea mammals and discuss several facts about each one.

Ages:
Advanced

Materials:
- *copies of the sea mammal clues provided in the activity*
- *slips of paper*
- *reference books*
- *chalkboard or easel paper*

Subjects:
Science and History

One of them inspired legends of beautiful mermaids. Another provided 18th- and 19th-century Americans with smokeless candles. And another faded into oblivion in the 1700s when it was overharvested for its meat.

These animals—the manatee, sperm whale, and Steller's sea cow, respectively—have all had an effect on people's lives through the years. And they've all been affected *by* people too. In this activity your kids can learn about these and other sea mammals by matching clues to the correct animals.

Start by writing the sea mammal names listed below on the chalkboard or on a large piece of easel paper. (Leave out the numbers in parentheses—you'll be using them later to check the kids' work.)

- bowhead whale (1)
- gray whale
- walrus (7)
- humpback whale (2)
- hooded seal
- harp seal
- West Indian manatee (8)
- orca (killer whale)
- monk seal (3)
- sperm whale (4)
- spinner dolphin (5)
- dugong
- Steller's sea cow (6)
- harbor porpoise

Next pass out copies of the sea mammal clues listed below. Have the kids write the names of all 14 mammals on the backs of their clue sheets. Explain that the clues fit eight of the mammals you listed, and six are "extras." Then tell them they'll be doing some "detective work" to figure out which of the mammals goes with each set of clues.

While the kids are doing their research, have them write a brief explanation for each clue that's marked with an asterisk. For example, the first clue in the first set reads, "fishing rods, corset stays, and umbrella ribs." The kids could briefly explain this clue by writing a sentence or two about the fact that the bowhead whale's huge baleen were once used to make these products.

When the kids have finished their research, go over their answers with them. (Each numbered mammal matches one of the numbered clue sets.) Use the information on the next page to discuss both the clues with asterisks and those without them.

SEA MAMMAL CLUES

1
- fishing rods, corset stays, and umbrella ribs*
- important to Alaskan Eskimos*
- despite protection, populations don't seem to have bounced back

2
- chirps, cries, and yups*
- the longest flippers
- endangered, but making a comeback in some areas

3
- warm tropical waters*
- endangered
- named for its loose neck skin*

4
- early American candles*
- machinery lubricant*
- *Moby Dick**

5
- acrobats*
- often swim with tuna
- sometimes drown in fishing nets*

6
- overhunted
- became extinct in the 1700s
- cold-water cousin of the manatee

7
- ivory*
- pale pink in water, reddish-brown on land*
- huge herds

8
- vegetarian
- motorboats often cause injury in Florida's waterways*
- mermaids*

Bowhead Whale

- In the 18th and 19th centuries, the bowhead's huge baleen were made into all kinds of products, such as fishing rods, buggy whips, ramrods, umbrella ribs, and stays for women's corsets and dresses.
- Since the 1930s, bowheads have been off limits to all hunting except that practiced by Alaskan Eskimos. The Eskimos have hunted bowheads for more than 3000 years. These sea mammals have been important to the Eskimos as a source of food. And the Eskimos consider the hunts an ancient cultural tradition.
- More than a century of vigorous whaling brought bowhead numbers down to a dangerously low level, and the mammals were finally given legal protection in 1935. Despite its protected status, though, the bowhead doesn't seem to be recovering. Scientists aren't sure why this is true, but some have suggested that this endangered species may be very sensitive to ocean pollution.

Humpback Whale

- These sounds are just a few of those made by the "musical" humpback whale.
- A humpback's huge flippers are about one-third the length of its body. Measuring about 16 feet (5 m) or more, they're several feet longer than those of even the largest creature on earth—the blue whale.
- Humpbacks were given legal protection in 1964. (Only subsistence hunters in parts of Greenland and the western Antilles are allowed to hunt these mammals today.) Recovery has been slow, but certain populations of humpbacks do seem to be increasing.

Monk Seal

- Most seals live in the cold waters of the far north or south—but the three species of monk seals are all adapted to the tropics. Hawaiian monk seals live on and around the chain of Hawaiian Islands known as the Leewards.
- Intense hunting in the 19th century for monk seal meat, skins, and oil depleted the seal population. Later, people moved into monk seal habitat when U.S. naval bases were established on the Leeward Islands (during World War II). The sensitive seals didn't adjust well to the human disturbance, and many abandoned their breeding sites for other, more exposed beach areas away from people. As a result, many seal pups didn't survive.
- The monk seal was named for the loose skin on the back of its neck. The skin looks like a monk's hood.

Sperm Whale

- Spermaceti, an oil found in an organ in sperm whales' heads, was made into smokeless candles in the 18th and 19th centuries.
- Spermaceti oil is still used today as a lubricant for machinery.
- Herman Melville's famous whaling novel, *Moby Dick*, was published in 1851. It centered on a hunt for a huge sperm whale.

Spinner Dolphin

- Spinner dolphins are well known for their spectacular leaping displays. They're named for the fact that they often jump out of the water and spin along their longitudinal axes. (Picture a spinning top or figure skater.)
- When tuna fishermen spot a group of spinner dolphins, they know there's a good chance that a school of tuna is nearby. Tuna often swim beneath the dolphins. Scientists aren't sure why they do this, but some think the dolphins' echolocating abilities may somehow benefit the tuna.
- Tuna fishermen often encircle schools of tuna with huge nets. If dolphins are swimming with the tuna, they might become trapped in the nets and drown. But new techniques are saving many of the dolphins' lives. For example, sometimes divers now help to remove captured dolphins.

Steller's Sea Cow

- The unaggressive, slow-moving Steller's sea cow was no match for people's weapons. Thousands were slaughtered for their meat.
- In 1768, just 27 years after its discovery, the Steller's sea cow became extinct due to overkilling.
- Steller's sea cow was related to the manatees and dugongs (the sirenians). But unlike these tropical species, the huge sea cow lived in the cold waters of the North Pacific.

Walrus

- Walrus tusks are made of ivory.
- When a walrus dives into chilly waters, its blood stops circulating through its skin and circulates only to its inner tissues and organs. This process, which helps to conserve heat, gives the walrus a pale pink color. When the animal crawls out onto land, the blood gradually flows back into the animal's skin, giving it a reddish-brown color.
- Walruses live in huge herds that often number as many as several thousand animals.

West Indian Manatee

- These "aquatic cows" and their relatives (the dugongs) are the only vegetarian sea mammals. They feed on sea grasses and other aquatic plants.
- The propeller blades of motorboats often injure (and sometimes kill) manatees.
- Many people believe that the legend of mermaids was started by sailors who (strange as it sounds) mistook these aquatic mammals for beautiful creatures that were half human and half fish.

Leonard Lee Rue III   walrus bulls

ODDS 'N' ENDS

rom egg-laying platypuses to armor-plated pangolins, some mammals are odd enough to really stick out in a crowd. In this chapter we'll take a closer look at some of these unusual mammal groups, which include platypuses, kangaroos, anteaters, armadillos, and others.

Incredible Egg Layers: *Monotremes* are real oddballs—they're the only mammals that lay eggs. Although they share this and a few other characteristics with reptiles, the monotremes (the duck-billed platypus and two kinds of echidnas, or spiny anteaters) are definitely mammals. The uniquely mammalian characteristic of producing milk for their young is a sure sign. But scientists weren't always so convinced. In fact, when a dried skin of a platypus was presented for study in the late 1700s, it was dismissed as a hoax. Even after the animal was discovered to be real, scientists were still unsure about how to classify it.

The monotremes live only in Australia (including the island of Tasmania) and New Guinea. (For more about monotremes, see "Egg-ceptions to the Rule" on page 26 of *NatureScope: Amazing Mammals—Part I.)*

The Pouched Pack: A kangaroo mother with a joey in her pouch is probably what most of us imagine when we think of *marsupials.* But there are over 250 species in this order, and there's a lot of diversity among them. For example, there are marsupial grazers (kangaroos), browsers (possums), insectivores (numbats), and carnivores (Tasmanian devils). There are marsupials that live underground (marsupial moles), in grasslands (wombats), and in forests (phalangers). There are marsupials that take to the air (sugar gliders) and the water (yapoks). There are marsupial "mice," "shrews," "squirrels," "badgers," and "dogs." There is even a marsupial "bear" (koala). And among kangaroos alone, there are more than fifty species—from the person-sized gray and red kangaroos to the small rat kangaroos. (For more about marsupials, see page 25 of *Amazing Mammals—Part I.)*

"Look, Ma, No Teeth!": What do anteaters, armadillos, and sloths have in common? It's not very easy to tell just by looking at them. But scientists group these animals together because of certain anatomical features they share. These three types of mammals make up the *edentates. Edentate* means "without teeth." But only the anteaters have no teeth at all.

Anteaters, armadillos, and sloths are found only in the Americas. The nine-banded armadillo is the only edentate that lives in the United States.

One-of-a-Kind: The aardvark, which is sometimes called the "ant bear," is similar in many ways to anteaters and was once classified as an edentate. But now scientists put this African mammal in an order all by itself. And it has the distinction of belonging to the only mammal order that has just one living representative.

Scales and More Scales: Scientists also used to lump the seven species of insect-eating pangolins (also called scaly anteaters) of Africa and Asia with the edentates. Pangolins are covered with overlapping scales over most of their bodies. They have long, strong claws like those of the edentates, and they can roll into a ball like some of the armadillos. They also feed on ants and termites, just as

colugo (flying lemur)

the anteaters and armadillos do. But because of their unique scaly covering and other anatomical characteristics, these "pinecone look-alikes" are now grouped in an order of their own.

Living Kites: Colugos (flying lemurs) of Southeast Asia resemble the primates called lemurs but are not closely related to them. Colugos have extensive membranes of skin (starting at the neck and connecting the ends of the limbs and tail), giving them the appearance of a kite as they sail up to 450 feet (135 m) from tree to tree. This characteristic and their habit of hanging upside down in trees make these odd animals seem batlike, though they're gliders rather than true fliers and aren't closely related to bats at all.

Midget Misfits: Hyraxes are small, rodentlike creatures of Africa and the Middle East. Scientists think that these unusual little mammals came from the same ancestral stock that gave rise to the largest browsing mammals on earth. So even though hyraxes look a lot like rodents, they're probably more closely related to the big browsers we call elephants!

anteater

platypus

aardvark

Oddball Options

Play a "describe-a-mammal" game that focuses on unusual mammals.

Objective:
Draw an unfamiliar mammal from a verbal description.

Ages:
Primary and Intermediate

Materials:
- *copies of page 71*
- *paper and pencils*
- *picture of a pangolin*

Subjects:
Science, Language Arts, and Art

 ere's a different way for your kids to learn about some not-so-familiar mammals. First pass out paper and pencils to the group. Then read the following description of a pangolin. Tell the kids to listen carefully to the description and then try to draw the animal based on how it was described.

> *This animal's body is oval-shaped and very wide. Its legs are short and thick, and its long, curved claws are tucked under its feet. Unlike many mammals, it walks on its knuckles. Its thick, pointed tail is as long as its body. And as the animal walks, its tail drags along the ground.*
>
> *The neck and head of this animal point downward from the body, making it easy for its long, thin tongue to lick up ants, termites, and other insects from the ground. Its neck is very short and thick and tapers into the head, which continues tapering into a narrow, pointed snout. The ears of this strange creature are almost hidden and its eyes are very small. And its entire body—which is about the size of a cat—is covered with thick, overlapping scales that make it look like a pinecone.*

When everyone is finished drawing, ask the kids if they know what the animal is. If they don't know, tell them it is called a pangolin and show them a picture of one so they can see how well their drawings resemble the actual animal.

Now tell the kids that they're going to get a chance to describe some unfamiliar mammals to each other. First cut apart some copies of page 71 and put the mammal pictures into a paper sack. Then have the kids choose partners and sit back-to-back. (Make sure the pairs are spread out so that they won't disturb each other when they begin talking.) Give one child in each pair a blank piece of paper and a pencil. Then have the other child in the pair choose one of the mammal pictures from the sack. (Remind the children with the pictures not to let their partners see them.)

Now have the children with the pictures describe their animals to their partners. The partners must listen carefully to the descriptions (asking for details as needed) and try to draw the mammals described. Afterward have them compare the two pictures to see how similar they look. Then have the kids switch roles, choosing a new mammal from the sack. When everyone has had a chance to try describing and drawing, pass out copies of page 71 to the kids so they can see what all of these oddball animals look like.

Note: Younger kids may have trouble describing the mammals well enough for their partners to draw them. To make things easier, pass out a copy of page 71 to both partners. Then tell the kids that they will be taking turns describing and identifying the animals on the page. First have one child describe one of the mammals on page 71 to his or her partner. Remind them not to say which mammal it is. Tell them to describe the animal's shape, fur or body covering, posture, and special features as best they can. Tell the listeners to try and figure out which mammal their partner is describing and to be sure to wait until they get enough information before they make a guess.

After they've guessed the right animal, have the partners switch roles. Have them switch back and forth until they've described and identified all of the mammals on the page.

As a follow-up, use the background information on pages 66-67 to talk about the mammals on the page and the things that make each one unusual or different from other mammals.

Pocket Pals

Make pocket-sized marsupials out of cardboard and burlap.

Objective:
Name and describe several marsupials.

Ages:
Intermediate

Materials:
- *copies of the patterns provided in the activity*
- *lightweight cardboard*
- *burlap (an 18 × 60" piece is enough for about 30 kids)*
- *glue*
- *fine-tip markers*
- *pipe cleaners*
- *scissors*
- *pictures of marsupials (optional)*
- *tape (optional)*

Subjects:
Arts and Crafts

The kids in your group can make their own marsupials to hang from or peek out of their pockets. First pass out a copy of the patterns below, a 6-inch (15-cm) square of cardboard, and a 6-inch (15-cm) square of burlap to each person. Then have the kids follow these directions:

1. Choose one of the pocket pal patterns and cut it out. Then trace the pattern onto the cardboard and cut it out.
2. Spread a *thin film* of glue *evenly* over the entire surface of the cardboard. Then stick it on the burlap square and let it dry.
3. Trim the overhanging burlap from around the cardboard. To make a furry-looking animal, leave about ¼ inch (1 cm) of burlap extending beyond the cardboard. Then unravel the extra fabric by pulling out loose threads. For a smoother mammal, trim the fabric close to the cardboard edge.

The glue will prevent the fabric on the cardboard from unraveling.

4. Use a fine-tip marker to draw the pocket pal's face and other features.
5. To make the opossum's tail, glue or tape a piece of pipe cleaner to the back of the cardboard and bend it into a curl. For the kangaroo, cut along the dotted line (see pattern) so that its head will be able to peek out over the edge of your pocket.
6. Hook the sugar glider's front paws, the kangaroo's head, or the opossum's tail over the edge of your pocket and take your pocket pal for a ride!

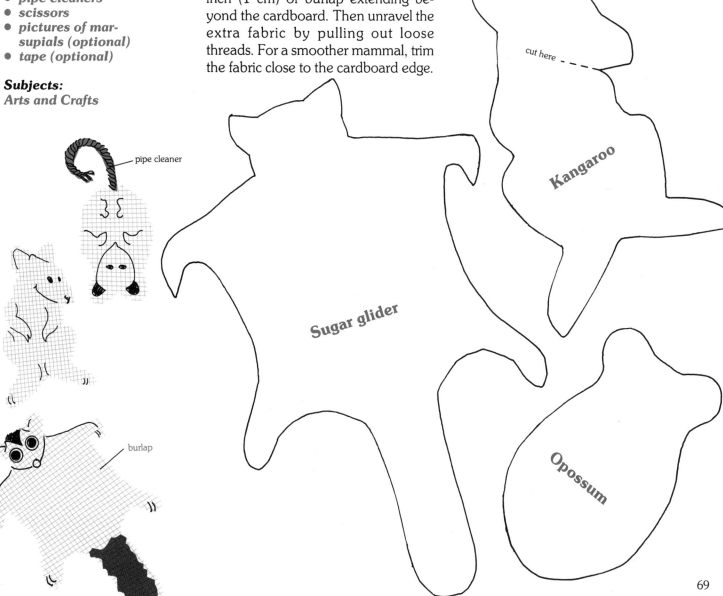

pipe cleaner

burlap

cut here - - -

Kangaroo

Sugar glider

Opossum

Fact and Fancy

Write a story that explains why some mammals look and act the way they do.

Objectives:
Define adaptation. Compare mammal adaptations for finding food and escaping from enemies. Write and illustrate a fanciful story that describes how a mammal adaptation came to be.

Ages:
Intermediate and Advanced

Materials:
- *copies of page 71*
- *copy of Just So Stories by Rudyard Kipling*
- *copy of "Why the Possum's Tail Is Bare" by James Connolly (Ranger Rick, April 1985)*
- *chalkboard or easel paper*
- *paper and pencils*
- *reference books*
- *crayons or markers*

Subjects:
Science, Creative Writing, and Art

In this activity the kids in your group can learn about some strange mammals by writing their own creative mammal myths. Before getting started, copy the suggested story titles listed at the end of the activity onto the chalkboard or a large piece of easel paper.

Begin by discussing some of the ways mammals and other animals are adapted to survive. Explain that adaptations are characteristics or behaviors that help an animal survive in its environment. For example, ask the kids to think about some of the ways a fish is adapted to life in the water. (Gills, fins, and a streamlined body are examples of a fish's adaptations for underwater life.) Ask them if they can think of other animal adaptations.

Next pass out copies of page 71 and tell the kids that each mammal pictured has special adaptations that help it survive. For example, the pangolin is covered with thick scales that help protect it from enemies. And the platypus has webbed feet that help it get around in the water. Use the background information on pages 66-67 to talk about some of the other mammals pictured.

Then ask the kids if they are familiar with Rudyard Kipling's *Just So Stories*. If not, explain that Rudyard Kipling was a famous author who wrote short stories, poems, and novels. He lived in India and England during the late 19th and early 20th centuries. In his *Just So Stories*, Kipling made up imaginative explanations that described how certain animals came to look or act the way they do. For example, "The Sing-Song of Old Man Kangaroo" is a story explaining how the kangaroo got its huge, hopping hindlegs and how it uses them to escape its enemies with great leaps and bounds. And "The Beginning of the Armadillos" tells how an armadillo got its armor and acquired the ability to roll up into a ball. (*Note:* Only three-banded armadillos, which are native to the region described in Kipling's story, can roll completely into a ball. The more familiar nine-banded armadillos—found in the southern United States and pictured on page 71—can only partially curl up their bodies.)

Read one or two of these stories to the kids. You might also want to read a myth that has been written by another author, such as "Why the Possum's Tail Is Bare" by James Connolly (*Ranger Rick*, April 1985). After reading the stories, discuss them with the kids. Ask them which parts of the stories are fact and which parts are fiction.

Then let the kids write and illustrate their own "just so" stories about one of the mammal oddballs shown on the Copycat Page. Explain that they can either choose one of the titles you listed or they can make up their own. Either way, their stories should focus on an adaptation of one of the mammals shown. Their stories should combine fact with fiction, explaining what the adaptation is really used for. For example, "The Beginning of the Armadillos" explains that the hedgehog and the tortoise changed into armadillos by borrowing traits from each other. This, of course, is fiction. But Kipling's story also explains that the armadillo has protective armor and can roll up into a ball to defend itself from predators—which is fact.

After they've finished, let the kids share their stories and pictures with the rest of the group.

Here are some title suggestions:
- How the *Platypus* Got Its Duck Bill
- How the *Sugar Glider* (or *Colugo*) Got Its "Wings"
- How the *Echidna* Got Its Spines
- How the *Tasmanian Devil* Got Its Pouch
- How the *Armadillo* (or *Pangolin*) Got Its Armor
- How the *Anteater, Aardvark, Echidna,* or *Numbat* Got Its Long Snout

young nine-banded armadillo

Leonard Lee Rue III

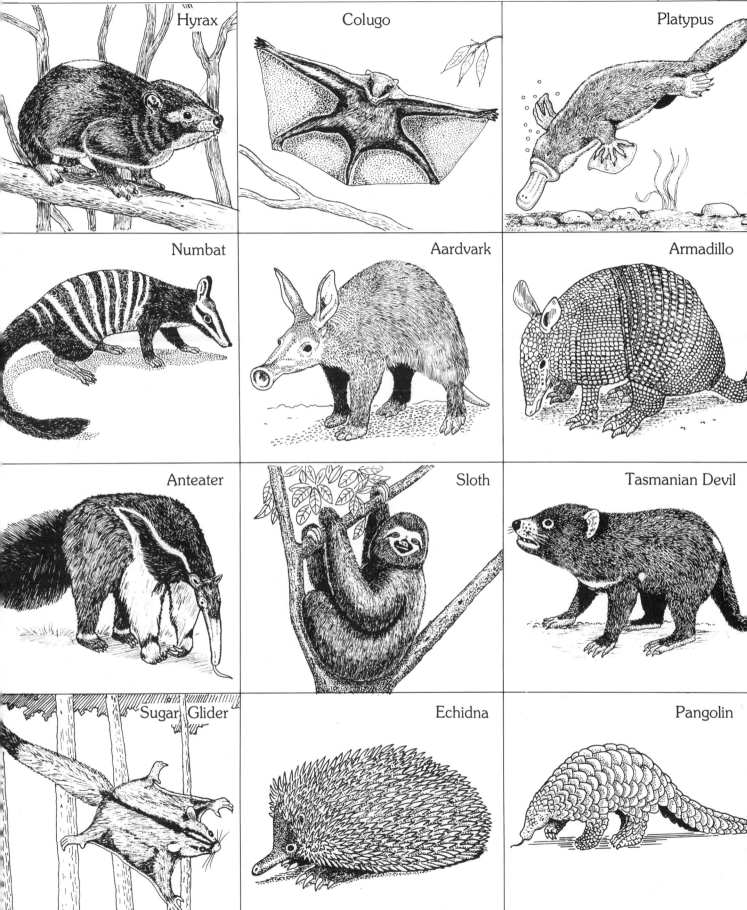

Hyrax

Colugo

Platypus

Numbat

Aardvark

Armadillo

Anteater

Sloth

Tasmanian Devil

Sugar Glider

Echidna

Pangolin

Glossary

wombat

baleen—gigantic plates, made of the same material as human fingernails, that line the mouths of some whales. These whales, called *baleen whales,* feed on plankton by straining sea water through the baleen.

blubber—a thick, insulating layer of fat just under the skin of many sea mammals' bodies.

carnassial teeth—scissorlike cheek teeth found only in carnivores.

carnivore—an animal that eats meat. Wolves, polar bears, and weasels are examples of carnivores.

cetacean—an aquatic, fishlike mammal that has paddlelike forelimbs and little or no body hair. Dolphins, porpoises, and whales are examples of cetaceans.

echolocation—a special hearing system in which an animal navigates or locates food by producing short, high-pitched sounds and then listens for the echoes the sounds make when they bounce off objects around them. Bats and dolphins are examples of mammals that *echolocate.*

edentate—a mammal that has only molars or no teeth at all. Anteaters, armadillos, and sloths are the three kinds of edentates.

herbivore—an animal that eats plants. Deer, kangaroos, and rabbits are examples of herbivores.

hindgut fermenter—an ungulate that has a relatively simple stomach and that ferments its food in an enlarged portion of its intestines. Elephants and all of the odd-toed ungulates are examples of hindgut fermenters.

insectivore—an animal that eats insects and other small invertebrates. Shrews and moles are examples of insectivores.

lagomorph—a mammal that has two pairs of incisors in the upper jaw, one of which is continuously growing. Rabbits, hares, and pikas are the three kinds of lagomorphs.

mammalogy—the study of mammals. A *mammalogist* is a scientist who studies mammals.

marsupial—a mammal that gives birth to tiny, undeveloped young after a short gestation period. The young attach themselves to nipples (often inside a pouch, or pocket) soon after birth, and there they finish developing. Kangaroos, koalas, and Tasmanian devils are examples of marsupial mammals.

monotreme—a mammal that lays eggs. The platypus and two species of echidnas are the two types of monotremes.

omnivore—an animal that eats a wide range of foods—from grasses and fruits to fresh meat and carrion. Bears, raccoons, and humans are examples of omnivores.

opposable thumb—a thumb that can rotate in such a way that its tip touches the tips of the fingers. Humans and most other primates have opposable thumbs.

pinniped—a carnivorous aquatic mammal with four flipperlike limbs, no tail, and a streamlined body. Seals and walruses are pinnipeds.

primate—a mammal that has several or all of the following characteristics: an opposable thumb, nails instead of claws, a large brain, and stereoscopic vision. Most primates live in groups. Lemurs, monkeys, apes, and humans are examples of primates.

retractile claws—claws that can be sheathed in an animal's paw. Almost all cats have retractile claws. Dogs, bears, and others have *nonretractile claws,* which cannot be sheathed. And cheetahs and a few other mammals have claws that are *partially retractile.*

rodent—a mammal that has one pair of continuously growing incisors in each jaw. Mice, beavers, squirrels, and many other mammals are rodents.

ruminant—an ungulate that has a multi-chambered stomach in which it ferments its food. Ruminants regurgitate their food and chew it a second time as cud. This process is called *rumination.* Camels, deer, giraffes, and all of the other even-toed ungulates are examples of ruminants.

sirenian—an herbivorous sea mammal that has a cigar-shaped body, a blunt snout, flipperlike forelimbs, and a large tail fluke. Dugongs and manatees are the two kinds of sirenians.

ungulate—a mammal with hooves. Horses, deer, and giraffes are examples of ungulates.

Questions, Questions, and More Questions

1. Name the three groups of sea mammals. (the *cetaceans*—whales, dolphins, and porpoises; the *pinnipeds*—seals and walruses; and the *sirenians*—dugongs and manatees)
2. Give three examples of adaptions that help sea mammals survive. (torpedo-shaped bodies, smooth skin or sleek fur, blubber, lots of oxygen-carrying red blood cells, fins and flukes)
3. What do ungulates eat? (plants and plant parts such as leaves, stems, fruits, flowers, seeds, bark, and twigs)
4. What is rumination and how does it help ungulates survive? (For an explanation of rumination, see page 26. Rumination helps ungulates digest and absorb nutrients from their diets of tough plant parts and enables them to eat foods that other animals can't digest as well.)
5. What's the difference between horns and antlers? (Horns are slow-growing, permanent bones that are covered by a layer of hard material. They are usually not branched. Antlers are fast-growing bones that are grown and shed each year, and they are often branched.)
6. What can bats do that no other mammal can? (fly)
7. True or false: Many bats can swim and walk as well as fly. (true)
8. Name three foods that different types of bats eat. (nectar, fruit, pollen, blood, fish, birds, insects)
9. Name two kinds of mammals that use echolocation. (bats, dolphins, shrews, tenrecs)
10. True or false: A shrew that hasn't eaten for six hours will probably die of starvation if doesn't eat soon. (true)
11. Which of the five senses do moles rely on most to find their food? (touch)
12. Describe a difference between rabbits and hares. (Hares give birth to precocial young; rabbits have altricial young.)
13. True or false: All rodents are smaller than a house cat. (False. Beavers, porcupines, and many other rodents are larger than a house cat. And the biggest rodent, the capybara, can weigh 140 pounds [63 kg].)
14. In which of the following habitats would you find a rodent: desert, savannah, forest, or tundra? (All. At least one type of rodent lives in each of these habitats.)
15. What are carnassial teeth? (scissorlike cheek teeth that help many carnivores slice through flesh)
16. True or false: All carnivores eat only meat. (False. Many carnivores eat insects and fruits in addition to meat. And some carnivores, such as the giant panda, eat mainly plants.)
17. Name two ways that play is important to a young carnivore. (helps it learn the rules of its social group, its rank in its social group, and how to hunt)
18. True or false: All cats have retractile claws. (False. The claws of the cheetah are only partially retractile.)
19. True or false: All edentates have no teeth. (False. Armadillos, anteaters, and sloths belong to this group but only the anteaters have no teeth.)
20. Name the only edentate that lives in the United States. (nine-banded armadillo)
21. Which group of mammals lives only in Australia and Tasmania? (the monotremes, which includes platypuses and two types of echidnas)
22. What's the main reason that many primates are endangered? (loss of habitat)
23. What's the most obvious difference between an ape and a monkey? (monkeys have tails—apes don't)

Move It

Objectives:
Learn what brachiation is and how it works. Research how other mammals are adapted to move in different ways.

Ages:
Primary and Intermediate

Materials:
- *Copies of pages 81 and 82*
- *Scissors*
- *Tape or glue*
- *String*
- *Crayons, markers*

Subject:
Science

Challenge kids to make a list of the different ways that mammals move (walk, run, jump, swim, fly, etc.). Which mammals do they associate most with each movement? Humans are mammals, so ask which ways of moving also apply to humans. Which do not? If a race were held between the best human runners, jumpers, swimmers, etc. and the best mammal in each event, who do the kids think would win?

Hand out copies of pages 81 and 82 and invite kids to make their model. (See below for instructions.) Do any of the kids know which animal is pictured? It is a gibbon, a kind of ape. Gibbons live in the rain forests of Southeast Asia. They spend most of the time up in trees, often more than 150 feet (45 meters) above the ground. Point out that gibbons are smaller than other apes. In fact, they are more the size of monkeys than the size of other apes.

How do your kids think gibbons get around so high up in trees? List their responses on the board. Ask kids if they have ever been on monkey bars in a playground. If so, how did they move from bar to bar? Did they ever move by hanging from a bar and using only their arms?

Explain that gibbons have long arms, flexible shoulders, and muscular hands that enable them to swing from branch to branch and from tree to tree. The sequence of gibbons in the model illustrates this mode of traveling, called brachiation.

Gibbons are expert, almost acrobatic, swingers. Note how they extend their long arms above their heads. They propel themselves along with well coordinated arm-to-arm movements while hooking their hands over branches. They can move so quickly that at times they seem to be flying. And they can leap more than 33 feet (10 meters) to escape predators.

At times, gibbons also walk along branches or vines with their arms held out for balance, like a tightrope walker holding a pole. They are adapted for this movement with opposable toes that grasp tightly to the branch or vine. (See Thumbless Relay on page 6 for a description of an opposable thumb.)

Divide the class into groups and assign each group either a mammal or a movement. Challenge the groups to research how that mammal is adapted to move or how different mammals are adapted to make the same movements. For example: how do beavers swim? How do kangaroos jump? How do horses gallop? How do flying squirrels glide? How do bats fly? Kids can compare mammals to other animals that move in the same way. For instance, they can find out if bats fly like birds or like insects, or neither. Allow kids to imitate the movements of different mammals by walking and running on four legs, jumping like a kangaroo, digging with their "forelimbs," and swinging with their arms as if through trees.

MAKING THE MODEL

1. Color and cut out all the gibbons.
2. Fold the flaps at the knuckles and tape or glue as shown:
3. Cut a string about 36 inches long and feed one end through the folded flaps so the gibbons are in numerical order. Tape the ends of the string across a door or window pane as shown:

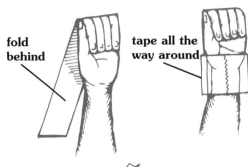

fold behind

tape all the way around

Home Sweet Home

Use dioramas to learn about mammal homes

Objectives:
Compare how and where beavers and prairie dogs make their homes. Research other rodent homes.

Ages:
Primary and Intermediate

Materials:
* *Copies of pages 77, 83, and 84*
* *Scissors*
* *Tape or glue*
* *Crayons, markers*

Subjects:
Science, Art, Writing Skills

Challenge your kids to describe any animal homes they have seen or know about. It need not be the home of a mammal. If kids can't think of any, start the ball rolling by asking where honey bees live.

Kids may wind up describing the habitat in which an animal lives because most animals live in the wild rather than in a home they build or in a particular place such as a tree hole or a cave. Why do kids think animals need homes? (Protection from predators, heat, cold, storms; somewhere to store food, sleep, raise young, etc.)

When it comes to mammal homes, few rival those of beavers as an example of expert building and prairie dogs as an example of community living. Invite kids to make the back-to-back dioramas of a beaver lodge and a prairie dog town (see below for instructions).

Using the labels to the cut-out pieces on pages 83 and 84 as clues, have your kids place these pieces in each scene wherever they feel appropriate and then write a story in the place provided on the stand-up piece about their diorama. If kids know anything about beavers or prairie dogs, allow them to include that information in their story. Or read the following paragraphs to the class before they begin putting the dioramas together.

BUSY BEAVERS

No wonder beavers are busy. These mammals have lots of work to do. With their chisel-like front teeth they cut down trees and strip off bark, leaves, and twigs to eat. They also collect branches to build a dam across a stream. As they build they plug holes between branches with mud

(continued on next page)

and stones. When the dam is complete, it holds back stream water. This water then rises and forms a beaver pond. Then the beavers collect still more branches and carry them to the middle of the pond, where they build a lodge. Inside the lodge there is a big, open, dry space above the water line with a small air hole at the top. There the beavers live and raise their young. Under water are tunnels just the right size for beavers to swim in and out of the lodge. Near the tunnel openings, beavers store extra tree branches as food for winter. They also collect mud and cover the lodge with it to prevent leaks.

In winter the pond may freeze over. The mud does, too, so no foxes or coyotes can walk across the ice and break into the lodge. Under the ice the beavers can still swim and reach their stored food. When spring returns, the dam and the lodge need fixing. A beaver's work is never done!

PRAIRIE DOG TOWN

Prairie dogs don't live above the ground but under ground in tunnels and chambers they dig. The tunnels and chambers make up a prairie dog town. Hundreds of prairie dogs can live in one town. They pile dirt around the openings to the tunnels, which helps keep the rain out. The dirt piles also serve as lookout posts. If one prairie dog spots a falcon, a rattlesnake, or some other predator, it barks as loudly as it can. This warns all other prairie dogs to dive into their tunnels. It's not only outside their town that prairie dogs must be on guard. Inside, burrowing owls, snakes, or other small animals may be lurking in tunnels or in empty chambers. Close to one prairie dog town there may be another and another. With so many prairie dogs around how can they tell where they belong? When two prairie dogs meet, they touch lips, open their mouths, show their teeth, and smell each other's scent. By this greeting ritual they can tell if they belong to the same town or are strangers. If they turn out to be strangers, they will raise their tails and keep sniffing until one leaves and returns to the town where it belongs.

Both prairie dogs and beavers are rodents. Encourage kids to find out more about both of these animals. Have them research the homes of other rodents as well as those of other mammals.

MAKING THE MODEL

1. Color all the pictures.
2. Fold page 77 in half so the printed sides face out.
3. Read the captions on page 83 for the beaver pieces. Cut out the front piece to the beaver lodge.

4. Attach the left side of the front piece to the beaver lodge as shown.

(continued on next page)

5. Attach the right side as shown.

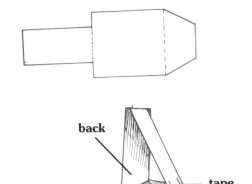

back   **tape**

6. Tape or glue the other beaver pieces to the front or main beaver scene.
7. Fill in the story on the stand-up piece.
8. Fold and tape the stand-up piece as shown.

9. Turn the diorama around and repeat for the prairie dog town and its cut-out pieces on page 84.

On the Tip of Its Tongue

Use a rhebus to find out about aardvarks

Objectives:
Learn how and where aardvarks live and hunt. Understand how aardvarks are adapted to capture ants and termites.

Ages:
First readers and reading challenged

Materials:
• *Copies of pages 85 and 86*
• *Crayons, markers*

Subjects:
Science, Art, Reading, Writing

Can your kids guess which is the first animal listed in the dictionary? Give them a hint that the first two letters in the name are aa. That animal is the aardvark. Not only is an aardvark a mammal but it is the only mammal that scientists place in an order all by itself. That's because the order has only one species—the aardvark.

Hand out copies of the aardvark rhebus on page 85. Go around the room and ask kids to read it aloud, sentence by sentence replacing each picture with a word or words. Then invite kids to make the model on page 86 of the aardvark capturing ants with its sticky tongue. (See below for instructions.) Also, hand out the paper and challenge kids to write a short rhebus story about the aardvark finding a meal of ants or termites.

AARDVARK FUN FACTS

If you wish to tell a little more about aardvarks, here are some facts:
1. Aardvarks dig up ants, tear into termite mounts, or lap up these insects as they march along the ground. Instead of destroying a termite mound, an aardvark first makes only a small hole for its tongue. Then night after night it returns to the same mound to enlarge the hole and feed some more.
2. An aardvark often walks on its claws when searching for food. It zigzags along, nose to the ground and ears pointed forward.
3. Aardvarks live on grassy plains, in woodlands, and on the African savanna.
4. To escape danger, an aardvark will dig itself into soft soil. It can dig faster than a person with a shovel.
5. The chamber at the end of an aardvark's tunnel is large enough for the animal to turn around in because they have been seen entering their tunnels head first and coming out the same way.
6. Aardvarks can't see well. People have watched them crash into trees.
7. If cornered, an aardvark will lash out with its powerful tail, strong legs, and sharp claws.

MAKING THE MODEL

1. Cut page 86 in half along the solid center line.
2. Color the aardvark pinkish-grey, then cut it out along the black line.
3. Fold the aardvark along the dotted lines as shown.
4. Tape the aardvark together as shown.
5. Cut the strip of ants along the three solid black line sides as shown.
6. Fold this piece in half along the dotted line and tape as shown.
7. Insert the X on the cut end of the ant strip into the front of the aardvark then out the back as shown. Tape the X end in place.
8. Move the aardvark to the front of the ant strip, then pull it slowly back so the aardvark's tongue can "scoop up" the ants.

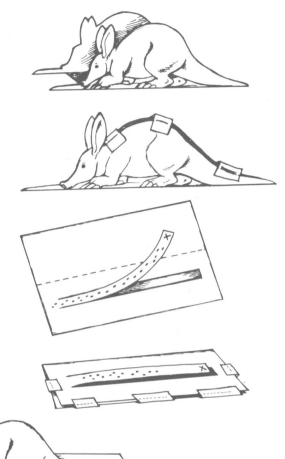

tape down here

Cats!

Make a field guide to cats

Objectives:
Learn about cats as examples of mammalian carnivores. Add written entries to complete a field guide to cats.

Ages:
Intermediate

Find out how many of your kids have or had a pet cat. Ask those kids to describe how the cat looks, how it behaves, what it eats, etc. Did the cat ever spot a bird or a mouse? If so, what did the cat do? Do your kids know about other kinds of cats besides house cats? Which ones? List their responses on the board. Which characteristics of these animals made kids associate them with house cats?

Cats belong to the order of mammals called carnivores. Nearly all carnivores hunt other mammals, birds, or fishes to eat. Only some, such as bears and raccoons, also eat plants and honey.

Like other carnivores, cats are armed with strong muscles, sharp claws and teeth, keen senses, quick reflexes, sensitive whiskers, and soft

(continued on next page)

paws for moving quietly. Cats stalk their prey, often hiding in ambush where their body colors blend in so well that the cats seem to disappear. Some cats, such as tigers, hunt alone. Others, such as lions, hunt in groups.

Like many other mammals, cats often claim a territory in which to live and hunt. They leave scents on rocks and bushes to mark their claim.

Photocopy pages 87, 88, and 89 and invite kids to make a field guide to cats. Explain that a field guide is a book with the names and pictures of animals and/or plants that live in different places. There are field guides to mammals, for example, as well as field guides to deserts, wetlands, and other habitats where mammals live. If you have such a guide, bring it in to look at. If not, try the library. Pass the field guide around and ask kids to read sample entries to give them an idea of the kinds of information they contain.

Note that on the pages you hand out there are pictures of eleven cats. Beneath seven of these there is text. If no field guides are available, kids can use this text as a model to fill in the entries under the remaining four pictures. Provide kids with books from which they can research facts for their guides. You can copy pages 87 and 88 in this book on carnivores or you may have to set aside time for kids in the school library.

Kids may want to focus on how one kind of cat is different from another, or how different cats hunt or raise their young. Invite kids to read their entries to the class. As you can see, one of the entries is on house cats. Challenge kids to use the information in their field guide to compare house cats to lions, tigers, etc. How are they alike? How are they different? Kids may want to create their own field guides to different kinds of house cats. Encourage them to do so, for this type of activity can improve how closely they observe animals and animal behavior. If you have access to a video of cats, such as lions hunting on the African savanna, bring it in. First show it with the sound turned down and see if your kids can narrate what the cats are doing and why.

MAKING THE FIELD GUIDE

1. Fold each page in half along the middle solid line, then in half again so the printed sides are on the outside.
2. Nest the three folded pages together so that the numbers are in order from the cover to 12. Pages 6 and 7 should be in the center. Pages 8 to 12 have neither picture nor printed text.
3. Staple the folded sheets in the middle as shown:

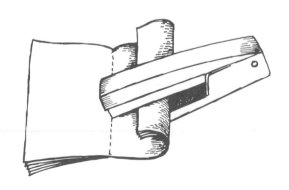

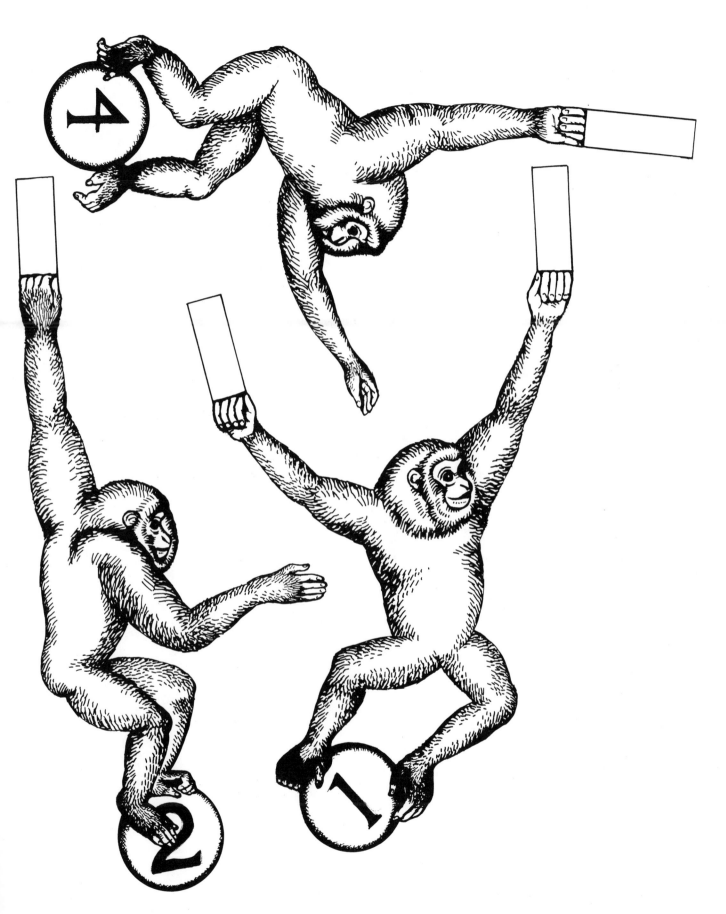

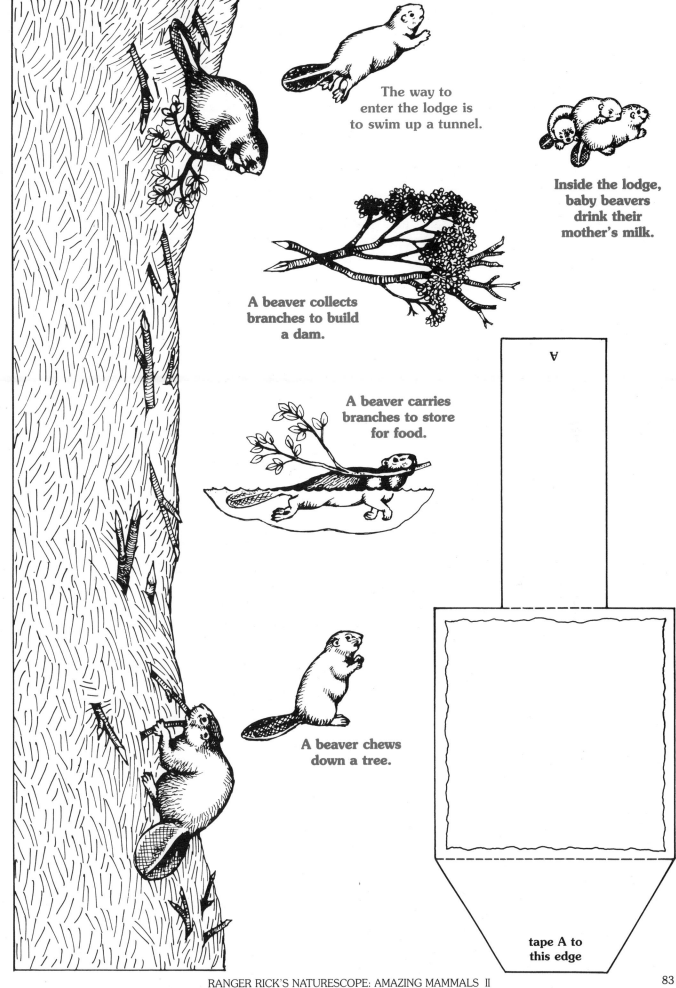

The way to
enter the lodge is
to swim up a tunnel.

Inside the lodge,
baby beavers
drink their
mother's milk.

A beaver collects
branches to build
a dam.

A beaver carries
branches to store
for food.

A beaver chews
down a tree.

A

tape A to
this edge

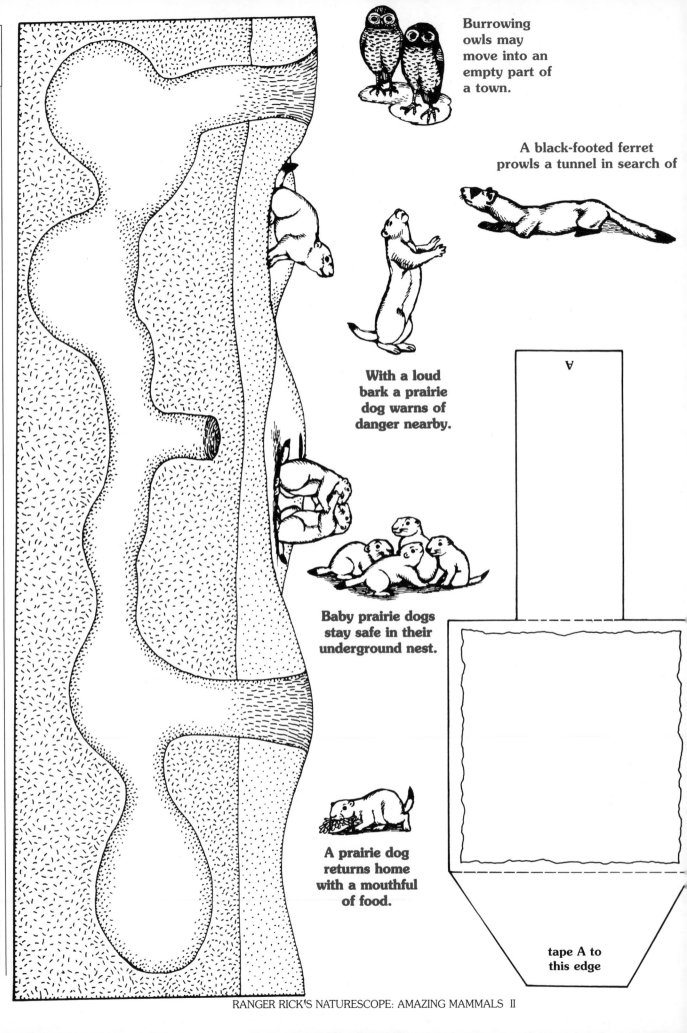

Burrowing owls may move into an empty part of a town.

A black-footed ferret prowls a tunnel in search of

With a loud bark a prairie dog warns of danger nearby.

Baby prairie dogs stay safe in their underground nest.

A prairie dog returns home with a mouthful of food.

A

tape A to this edge

RANGER RICK'S NATURESCOPE: AMAZING MAMMALS II

THE AARDVARK

An  hunts and termites at  .

It can smell these insects with its big . It can hear them with its big

When it finds an or termite nest, it digs a hole in it with its sharp

Then it sticks in its long, sticky and scoops out all the insects it can eat.

An  digs a long  big enough to turn around in.

When it digs, it closes its to keep out dirt.

During the day it sleeps inside the tunnel curled up in a  .

A mother  has **1** or **2** .

She protects them from a hungry  or  .

An  can grow **6** feet long.

It lives in where its name means +  .

But it is also called an +  .

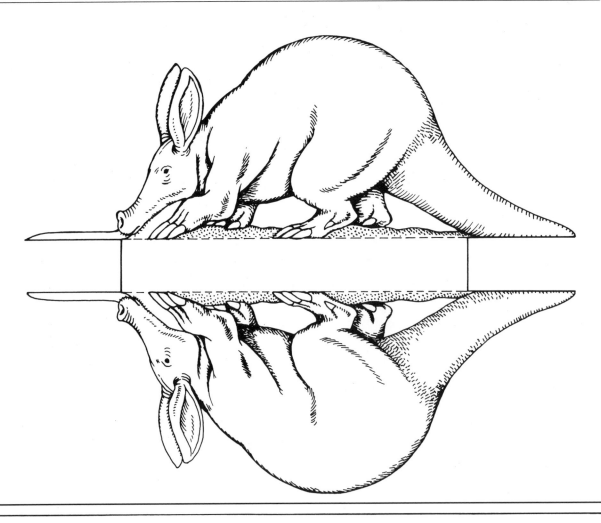

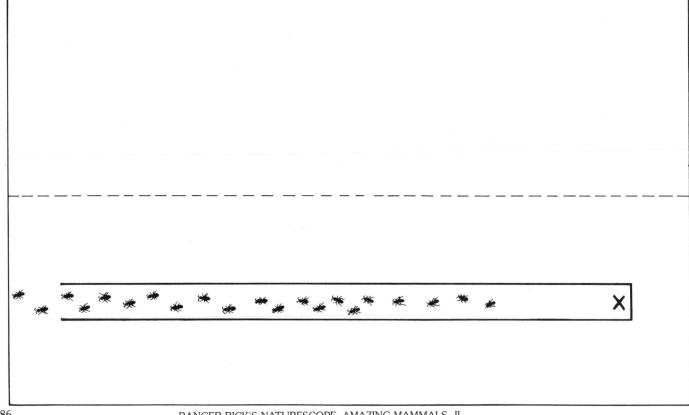

The high mountains of Central Asia are home to the snow leopard. There, this cat often dens in caves and stalks wild sheep, goats, and deer. Thick, furry, paw cushions help the leopard move over snow without sinking. Snow leopards are endangered species. Even though laws protect these cats, they are still being hunted.

SNOW LEOPARD

TIGER

COUGAR

_____

_____

_____

CHEETAH

No other mammals can run faster than a cheetah. This cat can sprint at speeds up to 70 miles an hour (112 kph). But it can't keep running this fast longer than a minute or so. After that it gives up and looks for another hoofed mammal to stalk. Cheetahs live in Africa and are endangered species.

LEOPARD

When a leopard kills a gazelle or an impala, it drags the prey up a tree. There the leopard can feast when it wants, away from hyenas and jackals. These scavengers might steal the leopard's catch if it were on the ground. Leopards live in much of Africa and in southern Asia.

CARACAL

With its long pointed ears, the caracal would be hard to miss. However, this cat is out mostly at night prowling for birds, rodents, and other prey to eat. Not only is the caracal a fast runner, but it is also expert at climbing and jumping. It lives in dry woodlands and savannas.

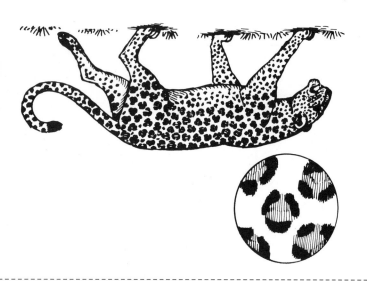

fold line

fold line

JAGUAR

Jaguars are the largest American cat. They hunt alone in woods, scrubland, and deserts for deer, birds, and rabbits. But they are also excellent swimmers and will prey on fishes and small alligators. Jaguars have been overhunted for their fur and are in danger of becoming extinct.

OCELOT

After a day of rest up a tree, an ocelot will climb down to hunt at night. Its keen hearing can pinpoint mice, hares, and snakes. Its razor-sharp claws and powerful teeth help it catch and quickly kill prey. Ocelots live in forests and scrub from Arizona to Argentina.

CATS

fold line

fold line

LIONS

Lions are big powerful cats that live on the African grasslands. They hunt by setting a trap. First some lionesses hide in grass. Then another female chases zebras or wildebeests toward them. The hidden females leap out, pounce, and kill one of the prey. Who eats first? The male lion who watched the females hunt.

BOBCAT

Bibliography

Please see *NatureScope: Amazing Mammals Part 1* for additional mammal resource listings.

(Note: A * at the end of a listing indicates that a book is a good source of mammal pictures.)

REFERENCES

General Mammals
The Encyclopedia of Mammals edited by Dr. David Macdonald (Facts on File, 1984). *
Walker's Mammals of the World, 5th edition, edited by Ronald M. Nowak (John Hopkins University Press, 1991). Two volumes *

Bats
America's Neighborhood Bats: Understanding and Learning to Live in Harmony with Them by Merlin D. Tuttle (University of Texas Press, 1988).
Bats of America edited by Roger W. Barbour and Wayne H. Davis (Books Demand, 1994).
Bats of British Columbia by D.W. Nagorsen and R. Mark Brigham, part of the Mammals of British Columbia Series, Volume 1, (British Columbia Press, 1994).

Carnivores
Cheetahs of the Serengeti Plains: Group Living in an Asocial Species by T.M. Caro (University of Chicago Press, 1994). *
The Cougar Almanac: A Complete Natural History of the Mountain Lion by Robert H. Busch (Lyons and Burford, 1996). *
The Great Bear Almanac by Gary Brown (Lyons & Burford, 1996). *
The Wolf Almanac by Robert H. Busch (Lyons & Burford, 1995). *
Wild Bears of the World by Paul Ward and Suzanne Kynaston (Facts on File, 1995). *

Insectivores
The Natural History of Badgers by Ernest Neal (Facts on File, 1986). *
The Natural History of Moles by Martyn L. Gorman and R. David Stone (Comstock Publishing Associates, 1990).
The Natural History of Shrews by Sara Churchfield (Cornell University Press, 1991).

Odds 'n' Ends
The Handbook of New Zealand Mammals edited by Carolyn M. King (Oxford University Press, 1990).
Kangaroos: Biology of the Largest Marsupials by Terence J. Dawson (Cornell University Press, 1995).
Koala: A Natural History by Anthony Lee and Roger Martin (New South Wales University Press, 1996).

Primates
The Natural History of the Primates by J.R. Napier and P.H. Napier (MIT Press, 1994).
Primates and their Adaptations 3rd edition edited by J.J. Head (Carolina Biological, 1987).
Primate Behaviour: Information, Social Knowledge and the Evolution of Culture by Duane Quiatt and Vernon Reynolds, from the Studies in Biological Anthropology, Volume 12, (Cambridge University Press, 1995).
Primate Life History and Evolution edited by C. Jean De Rousseau, from the Monographs in Primatology, Volume 14, (Wiley, 1990).
Primates of the World by Rod Preston-Mafham and Ken Preston-Mafham (Facts on File, 1992).

Rodents and Other Gnawers
The Black-tailed Prairie Dog: Social Life of a Burrowing Mammal by John L. Hoogland (University of Chicago Press, 1995). *
Marmots Social Behavior and Ecology by David P. Barash (Stanford University Press, 1989). *
North American Porcupine by Uldis Roze (Smithsonian Institution, 1989). *

Mammals of the Sea
The Book of Whales by Richard Ellis (Knopf, 1985). *
The Lives of Whales and Dolphins by Richard C. Connor and Dawn Micklethwaite Peterson (Henry Holt & Co., 1994). *
Seals and Sea Lions of the World by Nigel Bonner (Facts on File, 1994). *

CHILDREN'S BOOKS

General Mammals
Amazing Wolves, Dogs and Foxes by Mary Ling, part of the Eyewitness Junior Series, (Knopf, 1991). Primary and Intermediate
Animals Born Alive and Well by Ruth Heller (Putnam Publishing Group, 1993). Primary
How to Hide a Polar Bear and Other Mammals by Ruth Heller (Putnam Publishing Group, 1994). Primary
The Really Fearsome Blood-Loving Vampire Bat and Other Creatures with Strange Eating Habits by Theresa Greenaway, from the Really Horrible Guides Series, (Dorling Kindersley, 1996). Intermediate *
Sierra Club Wildlife Library: Great Mammals by Linsay Knight (Sierra Club, 1992). Intermediate and Advanced *

Bats
Bat by Caroline Arnold, part of the Animal Favorites Series, (Morrow, 1996). Intermediate *
Bats! by Ron Cole, part of the Ranger Rick's® Science Spectacular Series, (Newbridge Communications, 1996). Primary *
Bats for Kids by Kathryn T. Lundberg, part of the Wildlife for Kids Series, (Northword Press, 1996). Primary and Intermediate
Bats: Swift Shadows in the Twilight by Ann C. Cooper, part of the Wonder Series, (Roberts Rinehart, 1993). Primary and Intermediate
Extremely Weird Mammals: Bats by Sarah Lovett (John Muir Publications, 1996). Primary and Intermediate *
How Bats "See" in the Dark by Malcolm Penny, part of the Nature's Mysteries Series, (Benchmark Books, 1997). Intermediate and Advanced *

Carnivores
A Bold Carnivore: An Alphabet of Predators by Consie Powell (Roberts Rinehart, 1995). Primary
Amazing Cats by Alexandra Parsons, part of the Eyewitness Juniors Series, (Knopf, 1990). Primary and Intermediate
Animal Lore & Legend: Bear by E.K. Caldwell (Scholastic, 1996). Primary and Intermediate *
Bears by Bobbie Kalman and Tammy Everts (Crabtree Publishing Co., 1994). Primary *
Bears by Diane Swanson, part of the Welcome to the World Series, (Whitecap Books, 1997). Primary *
Bears, Bears, Bears by Wayne Lynch (Firefly Books, 1995). Intermediate and Advanced *
Big Cats by Bobbie Kalman and Tammy Everts (Crabtree Publishing Co., 1994). Primary *
Big Cats by Seymour Simon (HarperCollins, 1994). Primary and Intermediate *
The Big Cats and Their Fossil Relatives: An Illustrated Guide to Their Evolution and Natural History by Alan Turner (Columbia University Press, 1997). Advanced
Call of the Wolves by Melvin Berger, part of the Ranger Rick's® Science Spectacular Series, (Newbridge Communications, 1995). Primary *
Cheetah by Caroline Arnold (William Morrow & Co., 1989). Primary *
The Everywhere Bear by Sandra C. Robinson, part of the Wonder Series, (Roberts Rinehart, 1992). Intermediate
The Fascinating World of Bears by Maria Angels Julivert (Barron's, 1995). Intermediate
The Fascinating World of Wolves by Maria Angels Julivert (Barron's, 1996). Intermediate
The Florida Panther by Alvin Silverstein, Virginia Silverstein and Laura Silverstein Nunn, part of the Endangered in America Series, (Millbrook, 1997). Intermediate and Advanced *
Fox by Caroline Arnold, part of the Animal Favorites Series, (Morrow, 1996). Intermediate *
Gray Wolf Red Wolf by Dorothy Hinshaw Patent (Clarion Books, 1990). Primary and Intermediate *
The Great Antler Auction by Susan E. Goodman (Simon & Schuster/Atheneum, 1996). Primary and Intermediate *
Grizzlies, by Emilie U. Lepthien, part of the A New True Book Series, (Children's Press, 1996). Primary *
The Leopard Son: A True Story by Jackie Ball and Kit Carlson (Learning Triangle Press/McGraw Hill, 1996). Primary and Intermediate *
Lions by Amanda Harman, part of the Endangered! Series, (Benchmark Books, 1997). Intermediate *
Lions and Tigers and Leopards by Jennifer C. Urquhart, part of the Kids Want to Know Series, (National Geographic, 1990). Primary *
Look to the North: A Wolf Pup Diary by Jean Craighead George (HarperCollins, 1997). Primary and Intermediate
The Lost Grizzlies: A Search for Survivors in the Wilderness of Colorado by Rick Bass (Houghton, 1995). Intermediate and Advanced
Mark of the Bear: Legend & Lore of an American Icon edited by Paul Schullery (Sierra Club, 1996). Intermediate and Advanced *
Mountain Lion: Puma, Panther, Painter, Cougar by Sandra C. Robinson, part of the Wonder Series, (Roberts Rinehart, 1991). Intermediate
Mountain Lions by David Petersen, part of the A New True Book Series, (Children's Press, 1995). Primary *
Otters by Diane Swanson, part of the Welcome to the World Series, (Whitecap Books, 1997). Primary *
Please Don't Feed the Bears by Allan Fowler, part of the Rookie-Read-About Series, (Children's Press, 1991). Primary *
Polar Bear Cubs by Downs Matthews (Simon & Schuster, 1989). Primary and

Intermediate *

The Polar Bear Family Book by Sybille Kalas (Picture Book Studio, Australia, 1990). Intermediate *

Polar Bears, by Emilie U. Lepthien, part of the A New True Book Series, (Children's Press, 1991). Primary *

Polar Bears by Wendy Pfeffer, part of the Creatures in White Series, (Silver Burdett Press/Dillon, 1996). Primary and Intermediate *

Running Wild: Dispelling the Myths of the African Wild Dog by John McNutt and Lesley Boggs (Smithsonian Institution Press, 1997). Intermediate and Advanced *

The Sawtooth Wolves by Richard Ballantine (Rufus, 1996). Intermediate and Advanced *

Sierra Club Wildlife Library: Bears by Ian Stirling (Sierra Club, 1992). Intermediate *

Sierra Club Wildlife Library: Wolves by R.D. Lawrence (Sierra Club, 1990). Intermediate and Advanced *

Tigers by Lesley A. Dutemple, part of the Early Bird Nature Books Series, (Lerner, 1996). Primary *

Tigers by Jinny Johnson, part of the Highlights Animal Books Series, (Highlights, 1991). Primary *

The Wolves by Brian Heinz (Dial Books, 1996). Primary

Wolves by Seymour Simon (HarperCollins, 1993). Primary and Intermediate *

Wolves by Diane Swanson, part of the Welcome to the World Series, (Whitecap Books, 1996). Primary *

Wolves for Kids by Tom Wolpert, part of the Wildlife for Kids Series, (Northword Press, 1990). Primary

The Wonder of Wolves: A Story and Activity Book by Sandra C. Robinson, part of the Wonder Series, (Roberts Rinehart, 1989). Primary and Intermediate

The World of the Polar Bear by Norbert Rosing (Firefly Books, 1996). Intermediate and Advanced *

Your Cat's Wild Cousins by Hope Ryden (Lodestar Books, 1991). Primary and Intermediate *

Mammals with Hooves

All About Deer by Jim Aronsky (Scholastic, 1996). Primary

Animal Lore & Legend: Buffalo (Scholastic, 1995). Primary

Deer at the Brook by Jim Aronsky (Morrow, 1991). Primary

The Elephant Family Book by Oria Douglas-Hamilton (Picture Book Studio, Australia, 1990). Intermediate *

Elephant Families by Arthur Dorros, part of the Let's-Read-and-Find-Out-Science Series (HarperCollins, 1994). Primary

Elephants by Amanda Harman, part of the Endangered! Series, (Benchmark Books, 1996). Primary and Intermediate *

Elephants by Cynthia Overbeck (Lerner Publications, 1981). Intermediate

Gerald the Giraffe by John Storms, part of the World of Animals Series, (Heian International, 1995). Primary

Giraffe by Mary Ling, part of the See-How-They-Grow Series, (Dorling Kindersley, 1993). Intermediate

Giraffes by Emilie U. Lepthien, part of the A New True Book Series, (Children's Press, 1996). Primary *

Little Big Ears The Story of Ely by Cynthia Moss (Simon & Schuster, 1997). Primary *

Little Caribou by Sarah Fox-Davies (Candlewick Press, 1996). Primary

Llamas by Emilie U. Lepthien, part of the A New True Book Series, (Children's Press, 1996). Primary *

The Return of the Buffaloes: A Plains Indian Story about Famine and Renewal of the Earth by Paul Goble (National Geographic, 1996). Primary

Rhino by Caroline Arnold (William Morrow & Co., 1995). Primary *

Rhinoceroses by Amanda Harman, part of the Endangered! Series, (Benchmark Books, 1997). Intermediate *

Sierra Club Wildlife Library: Elephants by Eric S. Grace (Sierra Club, 1993). Intermediate and Advanced *

Zebras by Emilie U. Lepthien, part of the A True Book Series, (Children's Press, 1994). Primary *

Insect Eaters

Badgers by Lynn Stone, part of the Wild Animals of the Woods Series, (Rourke Press, 1995). Primary and Intermediate

Hedgehog by Western Promotional Books Staff, Nature Shape Books (Western Publishing, 1993). Primary

Skunks by Emilie U. Lepthien, part of the A New True Books Series, (Children's Press, 1993). Primary

Odds 'n' Ends

A Koala is not a Bear! by Bobbie Kalman and Hannelore Sotzek (Crabtree Publishing Co., 1997). Primary *

Amazing Animals of Australia (National Geographic, 1985). Intermediate and Advanced

Ever Heard of An Aardwolf? by Madeline Moser (Harcourt, 1996). Primary

*

Giant Pandas: Gifts from China by Allan Fowler, part of the Rookie-Read-About Series, (Children's Press, 1995). Primary *

Kangaroos, by Emilie U. Lepthien, part of the A New True Book Series, (Children's Press, 1995). Primary *

Kelly the Kangaroo by John Storms, part of the World of Animals Series, (Heian International, 1994). Primary

Pandas by Jinny Johnson, part of the Highlights Animal Books Series, (Highlights, 1991). Primary *

Pandas for Kids by Kathy Feeney, part of the Wildlife for Kids Series, (Northword Press, 1997). Primary

Primates

Extremely Weird Mammals: Primates by Sarah Lovett (John Muir Publications, 1996). Primary *

Eyewitness Books: Gorilla by Ian Redmond (Dorling Kindersley, 1995). Intermediate

Gentle Gorillas and other Apes by Allan Fowler, part of the Rookie-Read-About Series, (Children's Press, 1994). Primary *

Gorilla by Robert M. McClung (Morrow, 1994). Advanced

Kishina: A True Story of Gorilla Survival by Maxine Rock (Peachtree, 1996). Intermediate

Monkeys Are a Lot Like Us by Allan Fowler, part of the Rookie-Read-About Series, (Children's Press, 1995). Primary *

Sierra Club Wildlife Library: Apes by Eric S. Grace (Sierra Club, 1995). Intermediate and Advanced *

South American Monkeys by Amanda Harman, part of the Endangered! Series, (Benchmark Books, 1996). Intermediate *

Two Chimpanzees Return to the Wild by Andy and Linda DaVolls (Clarion, 1994). Primary

Rodents and Other Gnawers

Animal Lore & Legend: Rabbit by D.L. Birchfield (Scholastic, 1996). Primary and Intermediate *

Beavers based on IMAX/OMNIMAX Motion Picture (Scholastic, 1995). Primary *

Beavers by Emilie U. Lepthien, part of the A New True Book Series, (Children's Press, 1992). Primary *

Naked Mole-Rats by Gail Jarrow and Paul Sherman, part of the Nature Watch Series, (Carolrhoda, 1996). Intermediate and Advanced *

The Prairie Dog by Sabrina Crewe, part of the Life Cycle Series, (Raintree/Steck-Vaughn, 1996). Primary *

Rabbits and Hares by Emilie U. Lepthien, part of the A New True Book Series, (Children's Press, 1994). Primary *

Rabbits, Squirrels and Chipmunks by Mel Boring, a Take-Along Guide, (Northword Press, 1996). Primary

Mammals of the Sea

All About Whales by Dorothy Hinshaw Patent (Holiday House, 1987). Intermediate

As Big As A Whale by Melvin Berger, part of the Ranger Rick's® Science Spectacular Series, (Newbridge Communi-cations, 1993). Primary *

The Birth of A Humpback Whale by Robert Matero (Simon & Schuster/Atheneum, 1996). Intermediate

Giants of the Deep by Q.L. Pearce (RGA Publishing Group, 1992). Intermediate

Harp Seal Pups by Downs Matthews (Simon & Schuster, 1997). Primary and Intermediate *

Manatees and Dugongs by Amanda Harman, part of the Endangered! Series, (Benchmark Books, 1997). Intermediate *

Orca: Visions of the Killer Whale by Peter Knudtson (Sierra Club, 1996). Intermediate and Advanced *

The Sea Otter by Alvin, Virginia and Robert Silverstein (The Millbrook Press, 1995). Primary and Intermediate *

The Vanishing Manatee by Margaret Goff Clark (Cobblehill, 1990). Intermediate

The Whale Family Book by Cynthia D'Vincent (Picture Book Studio, Australia, 1992). Intermediate *

Whales by Amanda Harman, part of the Endangered! Series, (Benchmark Books, 1996). Intermediate *

Whales and Other Sea Mammals by Elsa Posell, part of the A New True Book Series, (Children's Press, 1982). Primary

Books in a Series

A First Look at Cats by Millicent E. Selsam and Joyce Hunt (Walker and Co., 1981). Other "First Look" books by the same authors are about dogs; kangaroos, koalas and other animals with pouches; monkeys and apes; and whales. Primary

CD-ROM & COMPUTER SOFTWARE

Animal Watch: Whales and Animal Watch: Wolves (both Intermediate) are two software kits from the *Explore-a-Science* series that include program disks, guidebooks and teacher's manual. Programs illustrate the habits and habitats of the animals through moving graphics. For more information write William Bradford Publishing Company, PO Box 1355, Concord MA 01742 or call 1-508-263-6996.

Voyage of the Mimi (Advanced) is an integrated program of videos, software and print materials involving math, science and reading. Students learn not only about whales, but also about navigation, ecosystems and beginning computer programming. For more information write Sunburst Communications, 101 Castleton Street, Pleasantville NY 10570-0100 or call 1-800-321-7511.

For Additional titles, please see the bibliography in **NatureScope: Amazing Mammals Part 1.

FILMS, FILMSTRIPS, SLIDE SETS AND VIDEOS

Ambush at Masai Mara (Advanced) is a video that focuses on a pride of lions. Write to Films Incorporated, 5547 N. Ravenswood Avenue, Chicago IL 60640. This title is available by special order only, so allow extra time for delivery.

Animal Classifications Series (Primary and Intermediate) this video series helps students investigate the world of birds, fish, reptiles and mammals. Titles include *If You Were a Mammal, If You Were a Reptile, If You Were a Fish and If You Were a Bird.* Each includes a teacher's guide. To order contact SVE & Churchill Media, 6677 N. Northwest Highway, Chicago IL 60631 or call 1-800-829-1900. Orders may be faxed to 1-800-624-1678.

Animal Families video series (Primary and Intermediate) introduces children to the habitats, life cycles and eating habits of many animals including *Dolphins and Whales* and *The Monkey.* Teacher's guides are included with each video. To order contact SVE & Churchill Media, 6677 N. Northwest Highway, Chicago IL 60631 or call 1-800-829-1900. Orders may be faxed to 1-800-624-1678.

Animal Homes 1st edition (Primary and Intermediate) these videos cover six different habitats and the animals found in each. Habitats include *The Antarctic; The Arctic; The Grasslands; Grassland Meat Eaters; Forest and Mountain;* and *Swamp* and *Marsh.* Each includes a teacher's guide. To order contact SVE & Churchill Media, 6677 N. Northwest Highway, Chicago IL 60631 or call 1-800-829-1900. Orders may be faxed to 1-800-624-1678.

Animal Homes 2nd edition (Primary) this program focuses on how some animal homes are constructed and how the homes are used by the animals for food storage, shelter and raising the young. Available as a video or as videodisc. A teacher's guide is also included. To order contact SVE & Churchill Media, 6677 N. Northwest Highway, Chicago IL 60631 or call 1-800-829-1900. Orders may be faxed to 1-800-624-1678.

Animals and Us (Primary and Intermediate) this videodisc provides basic information about animals and people. Topics include instinct, predation, animal homes, animal behavior, and the difference between mammals and birds. A teacher's guide is also included. To order contact SVE & Churchill Media, 6677 N. Northwest Highway, Chicago IL 60631 or call 1-800-829-1900. Orders may be faxed to 1-800-624-1678.

Animals, Animals filmstrip set with teacher's guide. Topics include migration, feeding and communication. To order contact SVE & Churchill Media, 6677 N. Northwest Highway, Chicago IL 60631 or call 1-800-829-1900. Orders may be faxed to 1-800-624-1678.

Animals in Spring and Summer/Animals in Autumn and Winter (Primary and Intermediate) this videodisc depicts how animals adapt to the yearly cycles of nature. A teacher's guide is also included. To order contact SVE & Churchill Media, 6677 N. Northwest Highway, Chicago IL 60631 or call 1-800-829-1900. Orders may be faxed to 1-800-624-1678.

Bat Conservation International has two shows available in slide or video format, *Bats: Myth and Reality* (Intermediate) and *Bats of America* (Intermediate and Advanced). For information write Bat Conservation International, PO Box 162603, Austin TX 78716 or call 1-512-327-9721.

Bears! (Primary) this video contains incredible footage of grizzly bears in Alaska along with interesting facts about them. A study guide is also included. To order contact Bullfrog Films, PO Box 149, Oley PA 19547 or call 1-800-543-3764.

Carolina Biological Supply has slide sets on many mammal topics including horns and antlers, endangered species and mammal predators. Each set comes with a printed guide. For more information write Carolina Biological Supply Company, 2700 York Road, Burlington NC 27215 or call 1-800-334-5551.

Earth's Natural Resources (Intermediate) this program explores our natural resources including wildlife. Available as video or videodisc. A teacher's guide is included. To order contact SVE & Churchill Media, 6677 N. Northwest Highway, Chicago IL 60631 or call 1-800-829-1900. Orders may be faxed to 1-800-624-1678.

Educational Images Ltd. has programs with cassettes and teacher's guides. Mammal titles include *Survey of the Animal Kingdom: the Vertebrates* (Parts V and VI) (available in filmstrip and video), *The Bison and the Prairie, North American Mammals, Water Animals* and *The Beaver's World,* all available as slides. For a catalog write Educational Images Ltd., PO Box 3456, West Side, Elmira NY 14905 or call 1-800-527-4264. They can also be reached on the web at http://www.educationalimages.com For email write edimages@servtech.com

Egg-Laying Mammals (Advanced) is a video that focuses on echidnas and the duck-billed platypus. To order write AIMS Media, 9710 DeSoto Avenue, Chatsworth CA 91311 or call 1-800-367-2467. Orders may be faxed to 1-818-341-6700.

Encyclopaedia Britannica has many mammal films including *Bobcat!* (Primary) and *Trail of the Buffalo* (Primary). For information write Encyclopaedia Britannica Educational Corp., 310 S. Michigan Avenue, Chicago IL 60604 or call 1-800-323-1229. They can also be reached on the web at http://www.eb.com.

The Great Canadians (Primary and Intermediate) video from the Kratts' Creatures television series presents information on the wildlife of Canada, with particular emphasis on the beaver. To order contact PBS Video, 1320 Braddock Place, Alexandria VA 22314-1698.

In Search of the Tasmanian Tiger (Primary and Intermediate) video from the Kratts' Creatures television series presents information on the wildlife of Tasmania. To order contact PBS Video, 1320 Braddock Place, Alexandria VA 22314-1698.

Junior Zoologist (Primary and Intermediate) this four video set provides a thoughtful introduction to the animal kingdom. Titles include *Mammals; Birds; Insects;* and *Fish, Amphibians, Reptiles.* Teacher's guides are included with each video. To order contact SVE & Churchill Media, 6677 N. Northwest Highway, Chicago IL 60631 or call 1-800-829-1900. Orders may be faxed to 1-800-624-1678.

Lion, King of the Beasts? (Primary and Intermediate) video from the Kratts' Creatures television series explores the relationship between predators and prey on the African savannah and discusses whether the lion is really "king of the beasts." To order contact PBS Video, 1320 Braddock Place, Alexandria VA 22314-1698.

Looking at Lemurs (Primary and Intermediate) a wildlife documentary about lemurs in Madagascar. Part of the Earth Creatures video series. Produced by Martin and Christopher Kratt, Earth Creatures Co. To order contact Bullfrog Films, PO Box 149, Oley PA 19547 or call 1-800-543-3764.

Mammal Slide Library is sponsored by the American Society of Mammalogists and offers 900 different color slides of over 600 mammal species. For more information, write Elmer Finck, American Mammalogists Society Slide Library, Emporia State University, 1200 Commercial, Box 4050, Emporia KS 66801.

National Geographic Society has many kits and videos. *Mammals and How They Grow* and *Whales* (both Primary) are *Wonders of Learning Kits* which contain a read-along cassette, teacher's guide, worksheets and booklets for 30 students. To order Kits or receive more information write National Geographic, PO Box 11650, Des Moines IA 50340 or call 1-888-647-6733. *Really Wild Animals* and *GeoKids* video sets cover a wide variety of animals. Videos may be ordered individually or as a set. To order videos or receive more information on them call 1-800-627-5162.

National Zoo: The Zoo Behind the Zoo (Primary) this videodisc introduces many animals found at the Zoo and gives a behind-the-scenes look at the people who study the animals and care for them. To order contact SVE & Churchill Media, 6677 N. Northwest Highway, Chicago IL 60631 or call 1-800-829-1900. Orders may be faxed to 1-800-624-1678.

Pan Troglodytes: An In-Depth Analysis (Primary and Intermediate) video from the Kratts' Creatures television series in which the Kratts brothers teach orphan chimps the skills they need so that they can be returned to the wild. To order contact PBS Video, 1320 Braddock Place, Alexandria VA 22314-1698.

Slowly Goes the Sloth (Primary and Intermediate) a wildlife documentary about three-toed sloths. Part of the Earth Creatures video series. Produced by Martin and Christopher Kratt, Earth Creatures Co. To order contact Bullfrog Films, PO Box 149, Oley PA 19547 or call 1-800-543-3764.

Squeak the Squirrel (Primary) video with teacher's guide about how a golden-mantled ground squirrel participates in problem-solving exercises. To order contact SVE & Churchill Media, 6677 N. Northwest Highway, Chicago IL 60631 or call 1-800-829-1900. Orders may be faxed to 1-800-624-1678.

Talking Forest (Primary and Intermediate) video follows various animals of the forest through the four seasons of the year. A teacher's guide is included. To order contact SVE & Churchill Media, 6677 N. Northwest Highway, Chicago IL 60631 or call 1-800-829-1900. Orders may be faxed to 1-800-624-1678.

Through Wolf Eyes (Intermediate) is a video about the social interactions of gray wolves as told by an elder of the wolf pack. Produced by Needham Gate Productions. To order call Environmental Media at 1-800-368-3382.

Tracks of the Grizzly, part of the Northwest Wild video series, (Intermediate and Advanced) provides information on grizzlies and how they differ from other members of the bear family. To order contact SVE & Churchill Media, 6677 N. Northwest Highway, Chicago IL 60631 or call 1-800-829-1900. Orders may be faxed to 1-800-624-1678.

The Way of the Bear in Alaska (Intermediate and Advanced) video discusses brown bear behavior. A study guide is included. Produced by Daniel Zatz and Derek Stonorov. To order contact Bullfrog Films, PO Box 149, Oley PA 19547 or call 1-800-543-3764.

Wonders of the Sea filmstrip set (Intermediate and Advanced) features animals and plants of the ocean. Titles include *Whales: Gentle Giants of the Deep; Sharks! Predators of the Deep; Boneless Creatures of the Sea* and *Animal Plants.* A teacher's guide is also included. To order contact SVE & Churchill

Media, 6677 N. Northwest Highway, Chicago IL 60631 or call 1-800-829-1900. Orders may be faxed to 1-800-624-1678.

BOOKLETS, KITS, MAPS

African Wildlife Dioramas to Cut and Assemble by Matthew Kalmenoff. For information write Dover Publishing Inc., 31 East 2nd Street, Mineola NY 11501 or call 1-516-294-7000.

Bat Conservation International has a large poster called "Bats of America." For information write Bat Conservation International, PO Box 162603, Austin TX 78716 or call 1-512-327-9721.

The Curious Naturalist, (Massachusetts Audubon Society, 1995). To order write Massachusetts Audubon Society, Educational Resources Office, 208 South Great Road, Lincoln MA 01773 or call 1-617-259-9500 x7255.

An Educational Coloring Book of Cats of the Wild (Spizzirri Publishing Co., 1983), ***An Educational Coloring Book of Mammals*** (Spizzirri Publishing Co., 1983), ***An Educational Coloring Book of Whales*** (Spizzirri Publishing Co., 1982), ***An Educational Coloring Book of Primates*** (Spizzirri Publishing Co., 1981) and ***An Educational Coloring Book of Marsupials*** (Spizzirri Publishing Co., 1986) by Linda Spizzirri. To order write Spizzirri Publishing Company, PO Box 9397, Rapid City SD 57709 or call 1-800-325-9819.

Krill is a card game about whales and other sea mammals and the roles they play in ocean food chains. For information write Ampersand Press, 750 Lake Street, Port Townsend WA 98368 or call 1-800-624-4263.

OTHER ACTIVITY SOURCES

Project WILD, developed by the Council for Environmental Education. Mammal-related activities include "Bearly Born," "Muskox Maneuvers" and "Oh, Deer!" To order write Project WILD, 5430 Grosvenor Lane, Suite 230, Bethesda MD 20814 or call 1-301-493-5447. Visit their web site at http://eelink.umich.edu/wild/

Rhode Island...Naturally program (Intermediate) has a curriculum on mammals with units on the gray squirrel, eastern chipmunk, white-footed mouse, white-tailed deer, little brown bat and opossum. A teacher's guide and reproducible materials are included. This is available to Rhode Island Audubon Society Workshop participants. For more information write Audubon Society of Rhode Island, 12 Sanderson Road, Smithfield RI 02917 or call 1-401-949-5454.

WHERE TO GET MORE INFORMATION

- College and university departments of biology, mammalogy or zoology
- Museums
- National Wildlife Federation's (NWF) Conservation Directory

NWF's *Conservation Directory* is the most comprehensive listing of environmental conservation organizations. Each easy-to-read entry contains all the information you need: names, addresses, telephone/fax numbers and description of program areas. The Conservation Directory is a valuable resource tool for people active in the field, students and adults looking for further information on various animal and plant species, and those seeking employment in natural resource management and conservation careers.

If you want to know the who, what, and where about environmental organizations, this is the book for you. The *Conservation Directory* can be ordered by writing to the National Wildlife Federation, 8925 Leesburg Pike, Vienna VA 22184. For discount pricing contact Rue Gordon at (703) 790-4402.
- Nature centers
- World Wide Web sites:
  Educational Images Ltd.
  http://www.educationalimages.com
  EE-Link Endangered Species information
  http://eelink.umich.edu/EndSpp/Endangered.html
  The Electronic Zoo http://netuet.wustl.edu/e-zoo.htm
  Encyclopaedia Britannica http://www.eb.com
  IWC(International Wildlife Coalition)
  http://www.webcom/wcwww/teachers_kit/learn.html
  National Geographic Society
  http://www.nationalgeographic.com
  National Wildlife Federation www.nwf.org
  Omnibus K-12 Science Server
  http://www.pen.k12.va.us/Anthology/Div/Charlottesville/
  SCHOOLS/CHS/RESOURCES
  Project WILD http://eelink.umich.edu/wild/
  U.S. Fish and Wildlife Service http://www.fws.gov
  U.S. Fish and Wildlife Service-Wildlife Species Fact Sheets
  http://www.fws.gov/~r9extaff/biologues/wildspp.html
  World Wildlife Fund fact sheets
  http://www.panda.org/research/factSheets/BrownBear/ index.htm
- Zoos

Internet Address Disclaimer:
The Internet information provided here was correct, to the best of our knowledge, at the time of publication. It is important to remember, however, the dynamic nature of the Internet. Resources that are free and publicly available one day may require a fee or restrict access the next, and the location of items may change as menus and homepages are reorganized.

Natural Resources

Ranger Rick® magazine is an excellent source of additional information and activities on many other aspects of nature, outdoor adventure, and the environment. This 48-page award-winning monthly publication of the National Wildlife Federation is packed with the highest-quality color photos, illustrations, and both fiction and nonfiction articles. All factual information in ***Ranger Rick*** has been checked for accuracy by experts in the field. The articles, games, puzzles, photo-stories, crafts, and other features inform as well as entertain and can easily be adapted for classroom use. To order or for more information, call 1-800-588-1650.

Ranger Rick, *published by the National Wildlife Federation, is a monthly nature magazine for elementary-age children.*

The EarthSavers Club provides an excellent opportunity for you and your students to join thousands of others across the country in helping to improve our environment. Sponsored by Target Stores and the National Wildlife Federation, this program provides children aged 6 to 14 and their adult leaders with free copies of the award-winning ***EarthSavers*** newspaper and ***Activity Guide*** four times during the school year, along with a leader's handbook, EarthSavers Club certificate, and membership cards. For more information on how to join, call 1-703-790-4535 or write to EarthSavers; National Wildlife Federation; 8925 Leesburg Pike; Vienna, VA 22184.

Index